THE SOLACE
OF ARTEMIS

First published in 2023 by
The Dedalus Press
13 Moyclare Road
Baldoyle
Dublin D13 K1C2
Ireland

www.dedaluspress.com

ISBN 9781915629159 (paperback)
ISBN 9781915629142 (hardback)

Dedalus Press titles are available in Ireland
from Argosy Books (www.argosybooks.ie) and in the UK
from Inpress Books (www.inpressbooks.co.uk).

Cover image: *The Peplos Kore* (Acr. 679), *c.* 530 BC,
photograph by Socratis Mavrommatis,
by kind permission of the Acropolis Museum, Greece.

Dedalus Press receives financial assistance from
The Arts Council / An Chomhairle Ealaíon.

THE SOLACE
OF ARTEMIS

PAULA MEEHAN

DEDALUS PRESS

Contents

꩜

MUSEUM

꩜

FOR THE HUNGRY GHOSTS

for Theo Dorgan

Sister Trauma

Brings me sage and dittany, brings me blue flowers —
Sits by my side in the blue hours

The curst path of my star for the misbegotten —
Her humours, her transits, her simples, forgotten

Shows me the mountain as medicine chest —
Says to walk this earth is to be twice blest

Once blest in Being: Once blest in Naming —
Shields of grace against historical shaming

MacCoitir, Mrs. Grieve, Culpeper, Galen —
Dog-eared old herbals of dearworts and dearbalms and dearbanes

She takes me by the hand to the very edge —
Her mysteries of cliff, of river, of littoral, of hedge

Sister Trauma offers me no choice:
The grave's long silence, her compensatory voice

The Ceremonials

The Solace of Artemis

I read that every polar bear alive today has mitochondrial DNA
from a common mother, an Irish brown bear who once
roved out across the last ice age, and I am comforted.
It has been a long hot morning with the children of the machine,

their talk of memory, of buying it, of buying it cheap, but I,
memory keeper by trade, scan time coded in the golden hive mind
of eternity. I burn my books, I burn my whole archive:
a blaze that sears, synapses flaring cell to cell where

memory sleeps in the wax hexagonals of my doomed and
    melting comb.
I see him loping towards me across the vast ice field
to where I wait in the cave mouth, dreaming my cubs about the den,
my honied ones, smelling of snow and sweet oblivion.

for Catriona Crowe

Alma Mater

They were taking down the elms when I was
first a student here — I walked through Front Gate
to sit at the back of Eiléan Ní Chuilleanáin's lectures,
being a back-of-the-class-girl, being a back-of-the-bus-girl,
being just gone seventeen and measuring
the teachers who would lead me towards the light
against my own inclination to be led astray.

They were taking down the elms — concentric rings,
the ripples of my life, like the long-playing vinyl discs
my music was graven on. The whole world rhymed for me
and I wore a dress of green velvet my mother
helped me sew — the elm's asymmetric leaves
chimed with its pattern of paisley. The song
itself was blind courage, the heart's true refrain.

Words, said the poet Pasternak, carry their own ghosts.
I see them daily in the babble of the city,
the weighted down-old women with their geist-bags of home
in languages I dreamt of when I was a child
watching satyrs chase nereids and naiads across
the snowfields of a tenement ceiling
bordered with panpipes, acanthus and orphic lyres.

I never knew we were disadvantaged till
they told us so in school, you could say
they beat it in to us, literally. We were told
we were stupid; I *knew* we were only poor.
But I was queen of every blossoming thing
I could name or hazard a guess to the meaning of.
Dear ghosts flocking like starlings to the elm branches!

The elms are down, and down their greeny shade,
their rugged bark where long-gone students carved their names
within a heart, and gone are all the moons and clouds and stars
once snagged in their rigging when I was finding my feet
and standing on them, my own two feet, shod in Doc Martens,
shod in sandals, ready to walk the songlines
of learning, ready to make an abiding song of home.

At the back of the class in the month of All Hallows
I heard that 'galaxy' contained the Greek word
for milk — gala! I could taste the Milky Way,
our cosmic mother sacramental on my tongue.
And tripped the light fantastic into verse —
the milk of human kindness, the milk of kinship,
the nourishing milk. Which brings me back to

alma mater, nursing mother, fostering mother, close kin
to Ceres, close kin to Our Lady, the medievalist's
Queen of Heaven, golden chain of memory, link
by shining link, that binds me to this place,
that lets me feel at home, a nursling at the pap
of human and non-human knowledge,
my nurturing metric, my compassionate mother lode.

for Eiléan Ní Chuilleanáin

Woman at Work

When I picture her now she is grinding
lapis lazuli in some scriptorium
by starlight, by her own light, in the shine
of the moon, mixing to a blue rapture

her sorrows, her angers. She is minding
her language, in the midst of alarums,
of sirens, of danger. She holds the line.
She sounds each letter, her song of water

fluid mirror to the cosmos above.
Like the ancient scribe snagged by a blackbird
who draws in the margins a feathery home

we've tracked through centuries this ferocious love,
stronger than the prescriptive word of any god:
where we build our nest, this edge we'll call *poem*.

for Ailbhe Smyth

#occupylanguage

Occupy language:
        the word truth
glistening like a new-born
           leveret in its form

Occupy language:
        the word justice
the scales of a rare beast
           rumoured extinct

Occupy summer:
        bee-loud abundance

Occupy winter:
        if it doesn't kill us
it will make us strong

And the leaves of autumn
        washing like grief
           to the floodplain

Occupy!

Occupy spring:
        if you dare
the mocking sap
      is a rising

Refusenik spring that occupies us

Occupy now:
        this moment's breath
is
        inspiration

And this moment's too
The universe occupying us

O occupy love:
          sing it with flowers
              to the waxing moon
Or whisper it through trees
              to the waning moon
bright bone in the morning sky

Occupy love:
          the pliant labials

Pitch your tent there
          among the blossoms of the city

Let it possess you
          seed syllable in the mind

Which mind 'altering alters all'

Old comrade, old heart teacher:

          love

Occupy peace:
          it will come
          'let it begin with me'
first step on the long march

Occupy space:
          its roof of sky
          Jupiter Venus
          Pluto making aspect

Occupy Saturn:
     its slow revolution come round again
making more precious
our eye blink span
on the home planet
Occupy language:
     reclaim the words
their sparking daemons
their electric charge

Reclaim night
     its mysteries

And day
     our own lovely star
warming our upturned faces

Occupy yourselves:
     your many selves
let them all flourish

Occupy silence:
     listen to its power

Occupy hope:

Occupy freedom:

Occupy language:

song for the longest night (dig the stillness)

my old friend
        still holding
                at the end
of a needle
        or a gun

too much dope
or not enough
the shadow on the wall
        the swinging rope

let's take the old road
        out of town
we'll stop by the woods

there's a fire path up
to a ring of standing stones

do you remember?
we went there as kids

we could lie there
under stars
our eyes open wide
pinpricks in the night

trace our mortal fate
        across the glittering chart

we could sleep
there at the heart
the moon waxing full

the deepest dreamless sleep

and wake at first light
to a new-spangled year

look back
along the trail

our track marks
          in the snow

the settling snow

The Merciful Hours

Because we have known Death come the hard way —
knock at the door in the dark of the night,
all of us breaking with the shock of day —

this precious time to sit with our living
while they enter their peace is pure gift.
It falls like healing light on our waiting

for heaven, or nothing, or another lifetime,
be we lovers, or father or mother
or child to each other. Our mortal dream

is to step out together the long road home,
hand fast in hand whatever the weather,
whatever the twists and turnings to come.

So: to the vigil bring candles, bring flowers,
heart's gratitude for the merciful hours.

At the Spring Equinox

I want to say it was a gearchange, the gales fitful
against new-born light, that creaking of the year into kilter.

The drudging out of winter, the near promise of summer,
when we ganged out around the rivers — the Wad, the Santry,

the desire paths to the Tolka valley, across the country
of their watersheds, Finglas Ballymun Glasnevin,

always the long way home. And sometimes we raised heaven
and sometimes we raised hell, those old pals, those dead mates

when we roved out, the children of the new estates
testing our futures, searching for the motherlode,

and we were forever singing, on the one road but not *their* road
whoever *they* were, as we roved out across the Finglas fields

to cut by Dubber Cross. Our guitars were warrior shields
when we roved out the backroads to the site at Ballymun

to climb down into the foundations with the setting sun
to wait the night come on with stars or cloudy skies.

I want to look once more into their clear or troubled eyes,
friends of my youth, to hear their beloved voices find the song

to reassure their shades that they belonged,
their every breath as good as every other

as we learned to make a verb of *to sister* or *to brother*.
I want to get down on my knees and kiss the ground

of their being. I want to spin them round and round
until we cease, with the towers above reeling

into absolute stillness — where comes a formal feeling
of complete ease in our teenage bodies,

dreaming of far-off fortune, fame, the alluring cities.
I want to feel their young hands gripped in mine,

skin on living skin, heart line to life line.
There are days when from memory I haul them up and out

and some days it's they who haul me up and out
when I hit rock bottom or contemplate the abyss,

when all my angels are angels of the apocalypse.
They reach me up into the stretched redemptive light of dawn

where we'll rove out by wet concrete, by hedges of blackthorn
through Albert College grounds and all our world

becalmed, enchanted and beguiled —
a blackbird singing in the fields of morning.

i.m. Chris Green

Old Biddy Talk

Have you no homes to go to …

The young mostly on one another's screens
— but these two rapt in each other
at the boundary wall: that genetic imperative,
the force that through the pandemic
drives their flowering, is my spring rain,
is my restorer from the deep-delved wells,
hauled to the healing light of this world
pure water tasting of gemstone & iron,
quartzite & gold:
        starlight & planets,
the sun & the comets, the moon herself,
she sacred to Brigit, mirrored in my bucket.
My breath, old spirit, stirring in the cowled
reflection of the earth geologic, old seas,
old forests wherein once we swung from tree
to waterlogged tree become shale,
become coal, become diamond.

          They are fire:
vestal and flame. They are immortal.

Old Fossil

a meditation on tautology in the Natural History Museum, Merrion Square

To spin the bitter word, the bad review,
the slagging in the blog I am reading,
to charm a lifespan with bright coins of luck:
the flip side of the putdown *old fossil*
is to be shrined forever in cold stone,
to be read as tail, as fin, as feather
in some natural history museum

in some far-off fin-de-millennium
fever, in apocalyptic weather
when this sad world is dust; and my vain bones
endure as sigils on the post-ordeal
sea bed, posterity's primordial muck,
like trilobite, like brachiopod, dreaming
calamite — eternity's daft voodoo.

Listening to Mícheál Ó Súilleabháin Play
'Carolan's Farewell to Music' on the Piano

In the stillness after
the last note resonates to nothing,
the light fades, November's moon waxes
over the rooftops
and night has all my care.

~

Amongst the shelved poetry books
I fancy birdlife prisoned in the leaves,
the dim memory of trees:
my workroom suddenly an aviary,
the poets' ghost warblers,
the chittering, chirruping, chirring, cawing, honking, clucking,
hooting,
tooting, murmuring, whistling, piping, trilling, shrilling,
twittering, tweeting,

the swan song.

~

I remember that 'truth' to the ancient Greeks
is literally 'not forgetting': and the word *swan*
does not forget it once meant *sound.*
mouth to ear, mouth to ear across the millennia
from the grandmother tongue.
Hence assonant, consonant, dissonant,
unison, sonata, sonic, sonnet —

my humble trade.

To write a farewell to music,
to be overcome with endings:
thanatography.

⁓

Once by a mountain tarn in snowlight
I watched nine swans lift from the water,
their wakes lapping the grasses at my feet
long after they were no longer
even shadows over the snowfield.

⁓

When synchronicity is flowing:
writing this poem and the postman delivers rhizomes
of the salt-tolerant anemone, *Wild Swan.*

I dream it next year Japanese in the garden
its white petals true windflowers,
feathery, yes, and angelic.

⁓

Digging out the compost in frosty weather,
mulching the beds,
Mars as close to us as it ever will be
in my mortal span.
In the voided time of Covid, I sweep the garden,
over my head five swans bronzed by sunset.
I vow to be peaceful, daughter of earth.

⁓

In from the orchard at dusk,
thawing my icy fingers at the hearth,
drying my mittens, my scarf,
I track the moonrise, her full face serene,
her maria and craters visible to the naked eye.

My hand too cold to write
I dream images in the flames,
the music of the settling logs,
murmurings from my bookshelves,
the poets restless.

⁀

Think in triplicities, in triads, in trinities:
to triangulate where you are in the infinity of time
take the last note of 'Carolan's Farewell to Music',
the solitary swan on Baldoyle estuary,
the last line of the last poem you will write.

Are you any the wiser?

⁀

Whatever wings that beat & beat & lifted
from this our broken earth
with the last mortal beating
of your heart
were bound for summer skies,
between the stars Albireo & Deneb
the full galactic nourishment
of the Milky Way.

⁀

I desire a music that is fractal —
as sure as the snowflake melting on my boot,
as sure as the pattern the ripple makes on water,
as sure as that swan's song,
the creature who carries our yearning across the generations,
heart and soul given in the art we are in bondage to,

before spirit lifts and leaves
your name in my mouth is prayer,
and the tarn's still water is mirror
to the fated constellations of our stars.

The Island, A Prospect

We learned that Ireland was a *temperate* island
from our first geography books, the climate mild,
the gulf stream a blessing that saved us from freezing
though we live at the same latitude as Moscow.
And the child I was found that word disappointing,
no earthquakes, hurricanes, typhoons, volcanoes, floods.
Temperate! A dreary wet city Sunday sound.

I took to astral travel out the school window,
lift-off on the storied wings of myth and legend,
and bitter tales of landlords and emigration,
of plantation, rebellion, famine and ruin.
They offered us a trope of the traumatised nation.
They made us feel the land had failed us. They bludgeoned
us with shame, left us lost, fearing our own shadows.

I grew up. I roved out in blue britches of denim.
I walked the roads. I slept in ditches. I fell in love
with a mountain tarn. Its black eye mirrored the stars.
The island took hold of me: ice-sculpted valleys,
glacial erratics, moraine, esker, bog, karst,
her meadows, her rivers; and beamed down from above —
Planet Earth — our grave mother as seen from above.

The mitochondrial tug of eternity,
that slow pulse of evolutionary regard
from deep within the ancient reptilian brain,
seat of instinct; from such a critical distance,
my neo-aboriginal imagination
must dream new endings, must fashion prophetic words
fearing they'll not be heard by our posterity.

Can we trust the visions teeming in the hours of trance,
knowing art is toxic (little arrows of guilt!) —
cadmium, chromium, cobalt, magnesium, lead?
To make paper is to make poison, no hand's clean.
All our craft work, all our magic, this we trade:
for bee music, music of otter, hare, kite, stoat,
the gold-nebbed blackbird's blissful song of happenstance.

Last week I walked to Feltrim in the pouring rain,
considered the redundant nature of its name —
Faoldroim, from the Irish, means Ridge of the Wolves.
The wolves are long extinct and half gone is the ridge
(its requiem the thud and blast of explosive),
limestone lorried away to serve that beast, the boom,
the turbo cycle over and over again.

High on Feltrim Hill Nathaniel Hone loved to sketch
Lambay and Ireland's Eye, the wild coastal fractals;
and Samuel Beckett's favourite view was down-
wards to Saint Ita's psychiatric hospital.
You're on Earth. There's no cure for that … our human span
an eyeblink. To save the world is not so simple
as to mine an ocean for each salt tear we've wept.

The Celtic Cross Spread Dictated to Paula Meehan by W.B. Yeats from the Other Side

PIED

When he got there, there was no I there
so well his life was hidden from the poems.
Between the natal horoscope and the last breath
was cast self's shadow and self's light.
The haws clotted on the winter branches
and seven black swans paddled downstream:
I fancied the poet himself entered my dream.

IN THE BODY OF A CENTAUR

Under a waxing crescent moon he came
to stand by me. We were heraldic:
if I was spread-eagled, he was rampant
on an azure field. We whirlpooled together.
I polished his hooves till my face shone in them.
He plaited my mane; he ruffled my feathers.
He proffered red rosebuds out of season, out of time.

IT'S AN ILL WIND

Dust devil, tumbleweed, rolling stone,
lizard, tiger tail, eye of Horus, clouds.
You name it we'll find a pattern for it
in the tattoo parlour on the night shift

where someone is inking the spiral nebulae.
Next door in the bookies they are laying bets
on who will start the nuclear war.

IN THE MOUNTAINS

I met a woman carrying a lamb.
Stooped she was, as though she carried the world.
She babbled of serpents and trinities
in old languages no one alive could speak.
I offered her water. She promised me wealth.
There was nowhere to spend it so far up.
Besides, what I really needed was health.

LOST IN FOG

The fog was so dense we could not see the path
ahead or the path behind. It was safest
to stand still and wait for a change in the weather
we were under. As if we had landed
from a different planet, abandoned by our mothership
and no way home. I would have wept to hear
any other creature. Wolves. Sheep. Birdsong.

IN THE NEAR FUTURE

Which is as remote as eternity
or any earthbound way to measure time
and given there's no fool like an old fool

the only foolproof stance is to sit in quiet
and blissful emptiness, in the here and now.
The sun will rise, the moon will set, and stars
will wheel in antique grace across the heavens.

A FRESH START

So often involves falling apart
at the seams, or cracking up, or breaking down,
and though we have crawled on our hands and knees
across the desert wastes, parched, assayed by vultures,
how well we understand true wealth is sapling,
a drenching rain on soil to plant it in,
a dream of bark, of foliage, of cool green shade.

THE PRAYERS OF CHILDHOOD

Though we stand in the judgement of others
in the glare of their probing scrutiny,
though they condemn from their moral high ground
and label us guilty, our prisons are self-made.
It only matters we forgive ourselves
as simply as we were once urged to forgive
those who have trespassed against us.

THE DOOR

Through which you glimpsed the stars, through which you wish
to enter or to exit, given time enough:

the door between the worlds. The sentry
in his jolly red uniform embroidered
with pentacles — does he beckon or gatekeep?
Better to act than to ask permission. Push hard.
The wind will bless your forehead. Coming. Going.

ANGEL

Tumbled from the heavens up above,
your wings redundant as a dodo's. How good
to plant your two feet on our world,
be they cloven, be they flesh and blood.
To smell the pines, to walk the teeming woods
to settle to the music of the sea
beating out your fate; mortal, radiant in earthlight.

for Roy Foster

The Premenstrual Emails

Like some crazed President, finger on the button
to blast or not to blast, to rock the boat,
to sink the ship, to leave the whole caboodle float
rudderless up the creek without an oar – cotton

on to yourself, forty years of it, 'wise wound'
my eye; certify me, crucify me, de-digitize
me, and, *Jesus wept,* help me realise
that when I'm wired to the moon, looney tuned,

is not the optimum time to write to publishers —
all ex-publishers now — politicians, gatekeepers,
those sentinels at Parnassus' lowest slopes.
Better score a resinous lump of high mountain dope

and put the few days down in naval (sic) gazing
spring cleaning, garden sweeping, Irish hashy dancing,
turn the phone off, lock the laptop up,
play chess, chew rocks, spit fire, get ripped, count sheep,

count blessings for the emails all unsent
instead of beating oneself up for the ones one did
send, to wit and by way of example: that rant
when asked to support a rock band — listen, kid,

the 'important' rocks I've supported, lifted, hefted in my hand
are as follows and in chronological order (of holding
not of age of rock, not being a geologist, though having
an amateur's interest in all the material world, a real fan):

a bit of Nelson's Pillar, a bit of moon rock,
a bit of the Berlin Wall, the provenance, alas, of all three, dodgy.

A gig that could have got me out of hock.
Or the time I emailed the minister, the podgy

one whose election slogan was *Don't throw it all away!*
to ask if she was going to eat *it* so, whatever *it* was.
And then the Christmas when N was weeks, we thought days
from death, and I asked how she managed to pass

as cheerful, that she needn't be so anam-cara-ish
it was okay to let go, and roar and put the anguish
out, the anger that I knew was what I sensed
beneath the trite and saccharine missives to her friends.

Or the one to the feminist scholar who asked *Is there
a glass ceiling in Irish Poetry?* Glass? Glass?
Granite, more like. And my own, my chosen task
is to chip my way sans serif, stroke by stroke, letter by letter,

even unto the final syllable of recorded time
when I'll chisel through to some light at last.
And no, there is none, can be no avant-garde — it's already
    been and past
when you read about it in next Saturday's *Irish Times.*

Then there was head-the-ball who goes on and on and on and
    on about
his work, as if it makes him holier than
us raft of dossers, the only poet in Ireland with a (tra-la) job.
I sincerely recommend he kiss whatever stone

it is that's antithetical to the Blarney Stone, one
that guarantees the Gift of Mute, the Gift of Divine Aphasia,
    of silence,
my arse in fact, a petrifying prospect, no pun
intended. All this vented spleen, this ire, this violence

in word and thought and *send* — and me a Buddhist!
A common snapper off of noses more like!
That poor woman who'd married a Meehan in the Midwest
of the US of A, I good as told her take a hike.

She'd researched our family tree and Googled relations
Did I know we were descended from Royalty?
From (just imagine) Philip the Impotent of Spain?
I saw red, or blue blood, and disabused her of her faulty

grasp of history, for which she'd probably paid
some scam artist so-called-genealogist, inept
in all but fleecing gullible Americans of their self-made
hard-earnedloot. We were in fact an insignificant sept

from the butt end of nowhere, a one-horse town
on the Sligo-Roscommon-Leitrim border —
one-horse! make that one bicycle — by name Ballinameen
a dreary gaff that if misfortunate enough to be born there

you'd be on the Dublin Road within two shakes of a lamb's tail,
shanks mare or spinning your starry dynamo
and tell me how Phil the Spunkless got the get up and go go go
to sire or distaff or to be on the ancestral ball at all at all with
    his own tail

firmly, or flaccidly more like, between his royal legs?
It beggars belief and thus I have myself to beg
to differ with you my long-lost Yankee cuz
and as for your friend, the college professor, does

he really think that I'll go to Ritzville at my own expense,
for the exposure, to read my 'challenging' poems to his students?
Ask a plumber to etc and I'm at least as skilled as that.
Am I a stripper? Am I a polar bear? That's how cold it gets

41

round here at this time of the month, even with a fury
that could melt ice caps, that elects itself judge, that elects itself jury.
I'm sick of it, dragging it round like a dead beast
carrion stench, my taste is bitter, me my only guest, me my feast.

At least I can relate to the humble worm,
recycler, life-giver, as I spew it out in verse, and what's worse
is this pain in here, a bounce-back curse
from the virtual zone, able to do me serious virtual harm.

Mea fucking culpa — best send this to god
the great prestidigitator himself, on-off fancy dancer
and bearer of unpalatable truth, old sod,
with an inadequate torch, like a jumped-up cinema usher,

o big banger, button pusher, screen idol, he who sent
his only begotten icon down to save us mere mortals
frantic at our keyboards pecking out the pecking order, at our portal
to the world wide web, not sure if we're hell-, or heaven-bent.

Some day soon I'll be past it all, spun through and out
to the other side, perned in the gyres, transmuted, turned
into the inner adult I know is lurking like a glimmering trout
somewhere in these shallows, the calm pool of my mind.

for Ruth McCabe

Seven Stanzas for the Magdalenes

While they were washing the stains
from the poor's dirty linen
I wrote in Miss Shannon's class
An Old Boot Tells Its Story;
while they were scrubbing the sweat
of sex, of fever, of blood,
the marks of labour, of birth,

of afterbirth, weeping,
flushing it all down the drain,
we recited the seven
times table, the mysteries
glorious and sorrowful,
cad a dhéanfaimid feasta?
the tri-coloured ribbon-o.

In two big pillowcases,
I'd lug the family wash
along Sean McDermott Street;
or in the new baby's pram
curtains and blankets and rugs
wobbled over the cobbles
the year I turned eleven.

I thought they were nearly nuns
if I thought at all about
the sad ones checking the wash,
their hands chapped raw and mottled,
their cropped hair, their hickiness;
how one with the bluest eyes
petted my head, said *good girl,*

good girl, when the one in charge
wasn't looking. My world was
dark and light, fearsome, dazzling
by turns. I can feel her hand
on my head, smell carbolic
and bleach, hear the undersong
of clicking rosary beads.

The Republic was young then,
we thought at last we were free.
With hindsight I write this down,
the convent closed, the Magdalenes
still without justice or peace:
they turn in their unmarked graves
or take their cause to the streets.

I roam the rooms of the past
where dust settles on the floors,
the statues have tumbled down
and with them our foolish faith
in stone, in plaster and paint.
I believe in this one truth
light sings to the breaking dark.

for Ethna O'Regan

In Solidarity

In solidarity
with the clouds which took the bare look off the sky the day
you died, you'll never die! Morning cargo on the wind that
smelled of the sea; with the gulls that flocked inland upriver,
stravaging past Liberty Hall, raucous, raucous, raucous,
in solidarity.

In solidarity
with the moon, the wolf moon of January, a lamp in the early
dark your last night on this earth, Venus, a diamond, studded
the night, Pluto in Capricorn, Death drew down the fatal night;
with all the planets and stars that lined up to light your path
in solidarity.

In solidarity
with the weather — who will forget the mildness of it, the last
days bathed in all that radiant light, midwinter sun hung in the
southern skies, as if stopped still, the solstice burning like a
flame for you; with our own lovely star of morning, our seven
stars on a field of blue, ploughing a sea of blue, our scarlet
banners high-streaked upriver, tattered flags of sunset
in solidarity.

In solidarity
with the people bereft by your passing, bearing the ordinary
weathers along with their grief, with the passage of time your
name will shine like a star in our private and our public
firmaments, banishing darkness; with time itself which brings
us to our senses, brings us to our knees, which teaches us
humility and our own true natures
in solidarity.

In solidarity
with the foggy dew, the waxy's dargle, the dicey reillys, the heart
of the rowls, the twangman, and the rocky road that led you
down through the songlines of Dublin to the river itself, the
seagull raucous Liffey; its smell, its swell, its angelus bells
ringing o'er it, its crescent moon above and the whole world in
a state of chassis
in solidarity.

In solidarity
with those who couldn't organize a piss-up in a brewery, with
the one who roared 'up the knocked down flats'; with those
who were elected chair and sat there through tedium and
tension of meeting after meeting where the soul of the city was
fought for and even sometimes won and done on behalf of
those who couldn't organize the proverbial
in solidarity.

In solidarity
with the children we have lost and who have yet to be born,
Janus who names the month of your death, looking both ways
at once; walking backwards into the future, remembering the
future, staring clear-eyed at the past, intuiting the ancient
lineaments of the ancestors in the month of the wolf moon
in solidarity.

In solidarity
with your dreams now that we inherit them, wearing the year
of your death like a union badge, wreathed in your dreams of
dignity and justice, like a mantle your dreams for the city, for
the people; with the people, always with the people
in solidarity.

In solidarity
with the hare. You were there for it. Elect it now your totem
creature, loping through the sky meadows over Dublin, away
off into eternity; leaving the beloved streets, the beloved faces,
the beloved songs
in solidarity.

i.m. Tony Gregory

Diamond-Faceted, His Breath

'Which is heavier — a ton of coal or a ton of feathers?'

My father's death lay on me like a feather;
his own hard-fought-for last mortal breath
was diamond in the radiant Samhain weather.

Light as the pages that fell from *The Mirror* —
TOXIC DUMP: BANK BILLIONS LOST: TEST TUBE BIRTH:
—my father's breath could scarce disturb a feather.

The going was hard at Dundalk, at Uttoxeter;
Red Era a horse he believed had some worth,
given the right ground, the right kind of weather.

The half-done crossword: ten across, eight letters,
daughter. Nine down, bold — no! — wild. Seven down, hearth.
The words themselves as light as any feather

I could carry every step of my future
on the smooth or rocky contours of my path
whatever the news, whatever the breaking weather.

In the hospice garden, a child's laughter
falling like dry leaves to the hard black earth
was my father's death — the weight of a feather,
as I roved out into the coming winter weather.

Portrait of My Parents on Their Wedding Day

A black and white photograph
outside Donnycarney Church taken
seventy years ago: something
in their eyes, something forsaken

calls to me across the years —
remember us   even as we sink
in history's amnesiac quagmire
rescue us from the brink

of nothingness — a lien or a *geas* to enshrine;
or so it seems.
They speak to me in such clear young voices.
Surely that day they dreamt

me already foetal
below my mother's overbrimming heart.
Behind me my sisters, my brother
shaping up to play their part

in this mystery — incarnate souls
bound by our journey through her
body. All of us gleaming
in the thoughtful eyes of our father.

I have them step out of the photographer's frame
and into mine,
as bravely as they stepped down the aisle
and out into hard sunshine,

their names across my lips in prayer
when I remember how they tried

to shield us from the cold, the fear,
the hungry dawns, the angry tide.

In the here and the now of this autumn
I paint them in colours
to slow the mind, the hand, to bring
our lived past into their future.

Ciss would be dead at forty-two,
broken bird in her pain-wracked nest.
Larry would soldier on to nearly eighty;
stoic, lonely, blest

in his bewildering grandchildren.
But today, hand-fast again,
they look into my workroom
where I'm mixing up a forest green

for her ferny bouquet.
Calyx of cobalt and lemon yellow,
then carmine lake for the four carnations
that rest on the pillows

of her small breasts. Outside
in the radiant October weather
the Brent geese cross the sky from shore to field.
Buoyant as a feather

in my work, I paint
the three speckled buttons of his grey waistcoat;
I paint their hypnotic pupils,
the lampblack of his morning suit.

I wreath her in pearly cascades,
her veil embroidered with silk threads

I render in minute brushstrokes.
I crown her with undreamt riches –

gold at her wrists, on her fingers,
burnishing her Holy Missal.
I imagine the space between their cupped palms
a sacred vessel

where our stars sing wheeling
constellations: Leo, Aquarius,
the sacramental void
where the night comes on and the moon rises.

On Baldoyle Estuary

Halloween — and the Brent geese
settling on the eelgrass uncovered
as the tide goes out; and the moon
rising while the sun sets,
both cupped a moment in the same sky,

and I could go down on my knees
to welcome the coming winter
that the geese have brought us
as they've brought us every winter since
the end of the ice age

to pray that whatever the season offers
of loss or gain, be it sweet or be it bitter,
that for you, friend of my youth,
there will be respite from pain.
So that when nearby a firework or a truck backfiring

startles the dog that frightens the geese
up into a noisy constellation
of dark stars,
I think of my long overdue phone call
and your last dose of chemo —

and before the flock settles further up the estuary
on the ebbing tide, I wonder
will their spring return to the Arctic circle
leave you amongst the living
or amongst the dead.

The First of February: Howth Head

I lift my face from the earth of the allotment,
from planting broad beans in a row,
eye to Ireland's Eye, the wheeling gulls
wakefollowing the trawlers leaving harbour.

A sheltered dip on the Head,
above the money, their vainglorious houses,
below the heather: granite bones
poke through.
                Hens scratch in the dirt

and bees mass at the mouths of their hives
waking early at the end of the mildest winter.
A man is fencing a place for the pigs
and the nougat smell of gorse mingles

with fresh dung from the ponies.
The old excitement, the old burial of grief
with each committed seed. And the lift
of spirit as I tamp the tilth snug.

Back sore, shoulders aching, hands toughening
up after months of paperwork and books,
the Mac's blue screen a nagging bully
on my desk.
             This is my happiness:

to be mucked up to the eyeballs
in Theo's cast-off ravelled jumper,
rooting in this soil for scutch and dock.
To walk clear of the virtual realm

into this moment when I lift my eyes
to that falcon hunting the ridge —
shadow of my muse falling before me
as I step free and certain into my form.

Ballad of the Fallen World

You were brother to me in the darkness
You were sister to me in my pain
You, friend, with the stranger's eyes
I never even knew your name

Outside the storm has gone over,
the ash has drifted to rest,
the earth has covered the broken,
the sun still sets in the west.

The gulls are heading downriver —
father of water, mother of rain.
A child kicks leaves in the gutter;
far off: lonely lonely singing train.

I soothe the child to sleep at night,
the story of a maid, a prison tower,
told over and over. Her braided hair;
her lover; her saviour.

No poetry after Auschwitz —
the learned philosopher's belief.
Poets went on making poems.
The empty doorway. Centuries of grief.

There are those who track the paths of stars
across the face of the earth;
those who calibrate the electron's spin,
who estimate its worth.

There are those who speak of angry gods,
karmic vengeance, immensities.
It's the ignorant, not the innocent, I fear,
spinning their sad simplicities.

I tell the child it's a mystery
why human creatures act as they do.
I show her the scales of history —
what's been weighed there and by who.

We sit and watch the stars come out
one by fatal one;
their light so old, the source is spent
that once were blazing suns.

> *You were brother to me in the darkness*
> *You were sister to me in my pain*
> *You, friend, with the stranger's eyes*
> *I never even knew your name.*

Gerald Dillon Sonnets

ARTIST'S STUDIO, ABBEY ROAD

My Trinities — three paintings in one frame:
the then, the now, the might have been, the line
between the father, the son, my holy ghosts
of all the lost and broken ones. I've made
of Dresden, Hiroshima, the bitter news
that beats down with the February rain,
a man, a book, an hour of blessed peace.

As surely as I know the rain will cease
I know there was an end to mortal pain
for the communists, the gypsies and the Jews,
for all damned as *other*. For fear they'd fade
from memory like their murderers' boasts,
I dedicate my freedom in this sign,
a shrine to peace, erected in their name.

THE UNFINISHED PAINTING

Last night I saw the painting in a dream
and though I was not in the picture plane
I was just offside, shackled foot to wrist.
A red fox crossed my path from field to wood,
a heavy snowfall dampened down the shunt
of camp-bound trains, the prisoners' hungry *caoin*.
The red fox looked me squarely in the eyes

to reassure me vision never dies
if rooted in truth. So paint what you mean
about *snow   tree   path*; and mean what you paint.
Though underneath the snow there's the shed blood
of those whose names I read from this sad list,
and from the forest echo howls of pain,
I trust the path I'm painting leads me home.

DOMESTIC INTERIOR

Of all the seasons in this basement room
it was yours I loved. Not that I let on:
in Belfast style I said you weren't the worst.
I curl up in the hollow of our bed —
your shirt's abandoned on the chair, your shoes
and socks lie like snoozing pets among the ruin
of our days. You were my sun, my moon, my stars.

And in truth you still are despite our wars.
I'll never take your holy name in vain.
If bigots kneeling in their shiny pews
should call the law down about your head
or if by your friends and family you be cursed,
I'll stand by you — heart to heart, man to man —
the yellow door secured against their doom.

for Colm Tóibín

Sufficient Technology

Kobarid, the Slovene-Italian border:
we take shelter from the heatwave in the cool
of the Museum of the First World War.

A tunic, heavy, khaki, in a glass case
with a helmet, identity tag, tobacco pouch,
a line of stitches zigzag across a pocket
above a rip in the fabric. We speculate — bullet hole?
a hole scorched in the thick wool by an ember
from a pipe? wear and tear? something sharp?
The stitching is crude; we supply swollen fingers.
The knot is huge, the tacking rough, each stitch
has its own slant and makes a crooked line.
Mended under fire, we supply, or eyes streaming
in the bitter cold of a night watch.

I am reminded of another row of stitches.
Years ago, another heatwave,
Washington D.C., the National Air and Space Museum.
In the *Apollo to the Moon* Gallery
moved to tears: the frailty of the craft,
the risk of the journey and how homely
the spacesuits Armstrong and Aldrin wore,
making first footprints on the moon —
those perfect hand-stitched buttonholes
knacky as the ones it took so long to learn
when I made my sampler book of stitches
long ago in childhood, the Central Model School.

So when you tell me, friend, that weeping
is the body's fastest way of shedding stress,
I come into an equilibrium — an equipoise

between my body's fear of flight, of men & war,
and my body's dole of mercy, the tears I shed

for what the human hand can do,
for what the human hand can undo,
for what the human hand can mend.

A Netchke for Barbara Korun

Coming down off the high mountain
tracing the Soca River from her headwaters,
we stopped at every roadside tourist stall
trying to buy a netchke.
                                    Between one year
and the next they'd disappeared. *No call*
anymore, nobody makes their own bread.

Like a language or a creature you only miss
when it's already extinct, or like some
implement banished to a shed or attic
not yet dusted down for a museum of folk life,
the netchke and its name might just as well
have been a stream fallen into a fissure in the karst.

They sold wooden spoons, chopping boards, plaques
and souvenirs with *Lake Bled* or *Greetings*
from Slovenia in hot pokerwork. No netchkes,
those hollow troughs of birch to knead dough in.

A cranky woman in her seventies or eighties
bent over nearly double, dressed in black,
minding her son's stall on the road to Bohinj,
hoked one out of a heap of discarded stock.
It was shop-soiled and mottled with black
spatters of damp mould, but we got it for a song.
It fit the curve of my belly perfectly.

That night we reached the sea, pushed through Strunjan
out past Trst. We slept to the pulsing waves.
The moon was gibbous and my spirit baby rocked
as I cast her off from shore into the current.

Sonnet for Gary Snyder on his 80th Birthday

To sit an hour in gratitude, the heart
opening to dustmote sunbeam deep shade
in this sequoia grove the mind expands
to the edge of the forest which is the edge

of mind where I see the enchanted path
in and through the teeming forest of childhood,
your poetry written on my empty hands,
the leaves, your pages dreaming a whole age:

its mysteries writ clear as a star chart
across the heavens — the trail you have blazed —
O to be alive! The blest holy land
beneath my bare feet, humble and privileged;

to follow after, to walk the same earth,
to get down and kiss the ground of your birth.

Gatecrashing

Having long considered the ceiling of granite
and each word I chisseled to scribe a path through,
having shimmied up the slippery shaft,
having stormed the shining citadel,
having tunnelled under the guard house,
having both run the gauntlet and thrown it down,
having discovered when I got there

that there is and was no discernible there there
I fledged my wings, stepped off the edge of the known
to soar above our Republic of elsewhere, where else
but the beloved city, the river, the park, all that carousel,
and in the sea roads the delicate marvellous craft,
the evening sky a deep rapture of blue,
and all the gates open, the wheeling stars, the fateful planets.

for Ciaran Carty

Taxi

When he asks what I work at,
I say *cleaner.*

He'll not tell me how to clean.
'Go on. I know you. You're the poet.'

'No. I'm a cleaner.
I clean houses.'

'You do, yeah. Do you know
what you should be writing about? Do you?

The bankers. That's what. The IMF.
The ECB. Those wankers.

And the IRA. The Real IRA.
The Cokes. The New IRA. That's what.'

> Last night I dreamt my sisters were flames,
> burning in the wind. Four bright flames.
> And then one blown out by the breath of god.

'That's what we want from the poets.
Poems about the state of the country.

I write a bit myself.
The best poems rhyme.

All my own poems rhyme.
I hate all this modern stuff.'

> My sisters dance up the mountain
> torching the gorse, the pines.

Bee, rat, fox,
running before the smoke.
My sisters laughing in the wind.

'Katabatic.'
'What's that you said, love?'

'The wind. Katabatic and free.'

Anti-hex

Imagining the worst,
the absolute worst, that could befall
family, friends, my own true love, not by an act
of nature, or random accident, but a pact
human-devil-spawned, that might enthral —
before we knew it curst

by the glamour evil
casts. I've seen, for instance, the allure
the fascinatrix holds against the drudgery
of the world, or the lizard-tongued begrudgery
of sly drunks, or the damage sober
vainglorious louts will

inflict on a life's work.
I've seen fine men and women brought low
and ruined by glamour from a mediocre source.
I believe now in enchantment as a real force,
an intervention in the earth's flow,
a singing of the dark

into being, powers
abused for malefic ends to wound,
to poison and to calumniate those I love.
This morning I decide enough is enough,
that a good start is to be attuned
to the seed that flowers

when a safe space is made.
And no grand gestures are called for here,
a simple turning once more to the task in hand
that I spell out between the water and the land —

if made well enough then who need care
whether yea- or nay-sayed?

It is all in the mind,
what I write now by the turning tide.
As the full moon comes up over the horizon
I bow before her, I make her sweet orisons —
word-mother, light-bringer, teacher, guide,
cold guardian of our kind.

for Rachael Hegarty

Wingèd Woman with Hound

One of the four Wingèd Victories, Fidelity, at the base
of the O'Connell Monument, at O'Connell Bridge, Dublin.

It is mostly the children who notice me,
year after metallic year, who look up to see

the most amazing thing: a wingèd woman with a hound.
Fidelity! To the children I am not bound

to stone and prisoned on my plinth; I rest in the stillness
between one human heartbeat and the next. A child can sense

that any moment I might stand, leap and gain the heavy air,
Between one bronze wingbeat and the next might hear

the barking hound, the whole kit and caboodle loud and clamorous
as the city howling, growling, snarling, its rush-hour crises,

its church bells pealing, the sirens alarming,
urgent in the everyday whirligig, while I sit at the still centre, dreaming

myself back to the cauldron,
dreaming myself back through the aeons of children

to seam of copper, seam of tin. To be cast as a Wingèd Victory
in the crucible that is History!

See my wingèd sisters with their wounds on show,
bullets from some nearby revolutionary bother, a hundred years ago.

Look up! There's the man we were erected to.
All pomp on his pedestal, above it all, who

most days is crowned with a feral gull
that shits with sweet abandon where it will.

There was a child, once, looked up and loved me
— she made my bronze heart beat in pity—

she grew to adulthood in a woman-fearing state.
Out of her eclipsed, ill-conjuncted fate

I saw her slowly trudge
her broken womanhood to the bridge.

She climbed up on the parapet. She stepped out. She plummeted
to the jade-green Liffey and was swept

out to the Irish Sea. Hers is the memory we are keeping.
my faithful hound and I. So if you see me weeping,

in the rain or when the winter snow melts from my brow,
then this much you should know:

it is the child I mourn for and not the abstract concept
in whose name, and in whose image, I was cast.

By the Autumn River

after Mohammed Bennis

For I have sat here too many lifetimes
Watching the wheeling heavens

Mirrored in the flowing waters
So long our journey from the village

So hard our journey, its lessons
And I could fish from my blindness

A childhood memory — the road before us
New then, and loss a foreign word

We will have aeons to learn
All the time in the world to unlearn

Fatima Mansions, 1987

The cool April evening,
the golden crescent moon
light stretched over the flats:
we stepped out of a meeting,

to smoke or to take a breath.
'Jesus wept', you said.
Whether about the meeting itself,
no more acrimonious than usual,

or the story of the youngfellow
who drove the robbed double-decker
onto the bonfire —
Was it last year? Or the year before? —

or the man from the Corpo
who was regretful and sour;
or the sad one in F Block
who'd barricaded her front door,

I never found out, before
Foley's dog broke the silence
of that rare quietude,
old angers stilled and something like peace

had us believe for a moment
that all the lost children
had beaten a path home
and were tucked up safe and dreaming.

'This was a farm once,' you said
as if looking out over fields

of cabbage and spuds, cows
in the lane. And then

'If you save one life,
you save the whole world.
There's nothing to say
that life can't be your own.'

for John Cooper

A Few Words for Paul Durcan

At a workshop once
in the heart of the city
north face of Mountjoy Square

a blackbird hit the windowpane
       and dropped like a stone.
I took it in my cupped hands

and felt its heart pulse out its fate.
I felt that pulse, it enter me
and mingle with my own.

      I went back inside
to my startled class
to set the students to their task

to slit the songbird's throat
to see what made it sing.

Robin Redbreast

We didn't think you'd see Christmas

Nor what would come of those broken blue eggshells
you found last spring on the studio floor
below the nest built on and into the bristles
of a bunch of my largest brushes clumped in an old bucket:

And the architecture of that knacky nest —
a base layer of dry leaves and small twigs,
an inner layer of coir purloined from the hanging baskets,
a softer lining of bright green moss
and hair — my own grey hair and the dog's.

And those two fledglings who made us laugh
though there was nothing much to laugh about —
they looked like they'd just got out of bed,
mussed and bewildered, their head feathers ruffled.

You read from MacCoitir that the robin's breast
was splashed by blood when he pulled the nails
from Christ's hands and feet, that in gratitude
Christ gave the robin eggs the colour of the sky.

That out of pity the robin brings drops of water in his beak
to the lost souls in hell, that the red of his breast
is a memory of the flames that singed him there.
That he covers up the eyes of the dead with moss and leaves.
That a cure for depression is to stitch a robin's heart
into a pouch and wear it around the neck.

These things you told me watching the surviving robin
singing from the handle of the wheelbarrow full of snow.

You were hanging by a thread, you said, living on a knife edge,
you said, it was like walking on eggshells, you said.

While the robin sang his heart out to the darkening sky
we stood together wondering just how long you'd take to die.

i.m. Louis O'Connell

Lämmergeier

That day walking the mountain above the cloud cover
you spoke of raptors in the juniper-scented air,

watching the lämmergeier, in all its jowly magnificence,
the bearded vulture; how it lets drop scavenged bones

on ossuaries, bare stone ledges on the mountain, to crack
the bones, to spill the marrow from them, to suck

it up to feed her chicks. Which is why she is earliest to lay
her clutch of eggs, sometimes directly on to snow. And this you say

with wonder, and with a flourish as if your knowledge
itself had conjured the breeding pair above us from the wattage

of the sun. Then how exactly the multi-bearded, multi-jowelled
creature called to mind a cranky poet we both knew; it fuelled

our hilarity from the Coll de So, the Pass of Sound,
down the wildflowered trail through mist to lower ground.

Away with the lämmergeiers became our code for the deranged —
those politicians, bureaucrats, board members, who resist change.

This winter I will paint the snow above your grave on canvas
gessoed white, and paint the shadows of the creatures as they pass,

animal, human, furred, pelted, as they tiptoe by your coverlet
    of snow.
Those wheeling lämmergeiers! Talon locked with talon as they go,

spiralling through the updraughts, perning in majestic light,
tumbling down the heavens, spinning in the ecstasy of flight.

i.m. Bernard Loughlin

Crossing the Threshold

When I was a girl I spent all of three months
in a fever hospital — a room on my own
far from the city street I lived on.

No visitors allowed, but sometimes my mother's face
at the observation hatch. She sent in a doll
costumed as a nurse in a cap and a cape with a little tin watch

pinned to her chest. And that doll became confidant,
perched on the locker, a patient witness
to my natter and jabber, the long days to endure

and the longer nights when the stars wheeled past my window
and I learned their patterned journeys across the heavens
though not what their journeys portended.

I called her Nurse Harriet after the real nurse who came
to tuck me in, with the last bedpan,
with the last dose of tablets, with the last thermometer,

with the last taking of the pulse, and the chance of a story:
what my doll did in the war, what she did in the Rising,
what she did in the trenches, in the rocket to Mars.

She was hero. She was avatar. In her cap
and her cape and her little tin watch perched on the locker,
taking my measure through the hot winding nights

of sickness and the slow unspooling weeks to wellness.
Those whorled fingertips on the thin skin at my wrist; that cool hand
on my head. I fancy I can hear my own blood

thrumming through my veins. I must have been lonely.
I must have been frightened. It comes back so clearly
this Covid spring wheeling into *Summer of 2020.*

My nieces are nurses, their beautiful faces
marked and welted by masks and visors,
their word purses full of medical phrases

from the Latin end of the dictionary.
The matter-of-factness of their going out
to night shift or day shift is to me the entirely miraculous.

When I ask what they'd say of their lives now,
this: how unnatural to say goodbye
through windows, Facetime, Zoom,

the machines ticking out their cycles; how we find new ways
to hold and be held; how we deepen in mercy,
in kindness. And this is routine! All this is normal!

They step over the threshold, outer to inner, inner to outer,
they ward off the darkness, they are bringers of light
to this world — its dazzling confusions, its crystal certainties.

They open the curtains wide to the bright star of morning
after long night, between one breath and the next,
on a blackbird still praising the earth in her turning.

Letter to Philip Casey from Agios Kirikos

Your doppelganger ganging down the gangway
today; along the pier a halt, a stutter in the flow,
your dark blue raincoat, your stick pegging memory
to my line. A wind out of the west — a zephyr —
loosed from a god's wind-bag ruffles your locks, tender wind
that warms the earth for spring blossoming, that kindles,
that feeds the funeral pyre, that births the ocean's white horses

in myth. But it's not you this morning. Passing the sad café.
'Make it new,' you'd say. 'Fuck Pound, what could he know,'
I'd say, 'of our lives. Make it old again, make it starry,
volcanic, magmatic, under so much pressure
it be obsidian; let forest be coal, be diamond.'
Adamant, in the way of young poets with our spindles,
our symbols, our blessings, our riddles, our curses,

our yarns. I am by memory gutted as if a bird of prey
had swooped into the quotidian, a shadow
on the mountain, and plucked apart my reverie.
Once, near the end, you gave me a peacock's feather;
radiant in firelight like some longed-for twinned
dharma brother, landed in East Arran Street, candles
and burning birch casting bronzed light on your verses.

⸙

I thought the spring would never come.
And though spring will never come for you again
You are in all my springs

And we rove out
Our manuscripts clutched
In childish hands

How innocent we were and wise
Beyond our years
How much we trusted

How much we feared
How lightly we carried
The weight of our years

I see you now, son of water,
son of river water, your white river
the Bann, flowing past Hollyfort, lustred mirror
to your childhood; in her shimmer, a glimmer
of all the great rivers ahead, their charmed daughters,
and you, bright maker, their beloved singer.

In dream you come to me overbrimming with health,
strong in limb, your eyes blazing with truth;
you are planting fruit trees, the loam a fine tilth;
as you dig, an orchard grows, flowers in your wake: wealth,
you tell me, is what we hold in common — it be kin, it be kith.

You were our polestar, our guiding light, a beacon
in the obscurity and loneliness of our worst season;
you held the line, you did not weaken;
you shine eternal now, lucid in some angelic region.

How often we spoke of destiny, the spinning wheel of fate:
sean nós, fado, rembetika, the blues — the weight
of suffering a covenant, a sacred obligation to create.

Come the moon in solemn metric patterned from deep trance;
come the stars, the wheeling stars, to join our gallant dance.

Come the weathers, old friend, of those days, that in your light
we live and die and love.

Empty Boots

My young students' boots
in a row at the back door.
So lonely. So tough.

Heaven on Earth

Cloud, stars, the white moon:
on my path home, a puddle
cups the winter sky.

Young Love

That Skerries winter:
you read me Ulysses
night after broken night.

Museum

Invocation

As old houses harbour ghosts, so do words.
Take *museum* which comes down from the Greek,
a place to put things that please the Muses,

a shrine or seat of the old goddesses.
What you find here might not be what you seek.
Rich, poor, citizen, commoner, lady, lord:

mortal trace made immortal by design.
Surrender as you enter through their door;
know all are equal here: in Time's brute trust

we are held — the quick, the dead, the blest, the curst.
Open heart and mind to those who've gone before,
to honour the Muses — virgin, mother, crone,

and hope to glimpse them ninefold in this house,
daughters of Memory, oracles of grace.

Of Natal Charts and End Games

Not the clock to measure time and tide, but the moon,
her waxings, her wanings, her track across the star-
spangled heavens, trining and sextiling planets
to net and land another whole incarnate soul,
to earth this karma in the shelter of the house.
Cellular mirrors celestial, the spinning globe
slows to rest with the mother's cries, the child's first breath;

while elsewhere in the house, a different room, a death,
a last glimpse of ceiling as the light fails lobe by lobe.
Upstairs someone dreams of walnuts, a new blouse,
someone makes coddle, snuffs a candle, humps coal,
sips Vartry water, tastes trace of phyllite, quartzite,
greywacke, shale, slate — bedrock lithographies from far-
off Wicklow — while Angelus bells ring out the noon.

to Urania — Muse of Astronomy

Her Dignity: A Restoration

Once it was simple and clear: the world a dreamspace
when we were children and wrote in our copybooks
an old penny, an old hat, an old watch, an old boot,
an old house tells its story. An old woman tells *hers*
now, walking backwards into the future, her eyes
wide open, peering through the air so thick with trauma,
to the girl she once was, skipping the shadowy world

into being with each thump of the rope, or curled
to a foetal crouch under the bed, adult drama
raging overhead. You, who write the histories,
write her in, write her up, write her down, before she blurs,
an image disturbed in a scrying bowl, that the brute
erosions of a State helmed by liars, helmed by crooks,
might not yet rob memory of her abiding grace.

to Clio — Muse of History

Children of the Wind

Where are they now, the children of the house, who flocked
like rooks at dusk, or gulls come in from stormy seas,
raucous through the rooms, from area up to attic
to nest in cribs, to huddle in beds, to dream in cots,
to rise again in the morning, to make the whole
world up, over and over, their voices piping,
puling, shrilling, in glorious cacophony?

They had no fear of time. Their ancient cartographies
still scribed in the walls, their seeking, their hiding,
their yo-yos, their piggy beds, their Ludo, their ... goals!
'I'm coming, ready or not, keep your place or you'll be caught.'
Their rhyming chants echo even yet. O my erratic
stars, that wandered the face of the heavens,
blown hither, blown thither, on cosmic currents rocked.

to Euterpe — Muse of Song and Elegiac Poetry

The Acoustic

As slowly as a tortoise, time moves through these rooms:
light eternal nuzzling up to windows and under doors,
ethereal music — a voice broken with desire
that plucks at the heartstrings. It sings of love, love lost
and hope abandoned. It sings of an empty bed,
of roses and myrtle withering in a glass jar,
of turtle doves, of snow falling to the garden.

They were much like us: they lived, they died on the margin.
The archive opens, a glimpse of who they were, star-
crossed lovers. Then slams shut again on the silenced dead.
We fare no better now than they once did — the cost
of love for some frail souls is a funeral pyre.
We'll keep on making songs, we'll sing through peace, through war,
our songs of lovers lonely in their vaulted tombs.

to Erato — Muse of Lyric Poetry

'Step We Gaily, On We Go'

Some nights when the moon is full, the ghosts come out to dance:
they reel and they jig and they jitter across the boards.
They clasp each other's spectral hands throughout the ages,
Republican shimmies with Ascendancy lady,
Militia Captain toe to toe with scullery maid.
They swing their partners while spirit music blares;
sage, fool, rich, poor, made equal in this Danse Macabre.

A rustle of silk, a rattle of tarnished sabre,
their shadowy shindig teeming up the backstairs
to trip the light fandango, beau and jade,
skeletal revenants grieving the loss of body,
remembering strong hearts pounding in rib cages,
blood rising, pulsing with the music's major chords
to possess the frenzied dancers in ecstatic trance.

to Terpsichore — Muse of Dance

This Bed, This Raft On Stormy Seas

The start of her lying-in was the end of mornings
at the pier glass, mouse-skin eyebrows, eyes outlined in jet,
cheeks rouged, got from recipes in *The Art of Beauty;*
gall-nuts, black lead, mercury, carmine, liquid pitch,
her glued-on beauty spots of taffeta and silk,
her drapery, her napery, her blue, blue walls.
Birth the leveller pays no heed to class, to kind —

our crossing fraught with peril to body and to mind.
In every generation there are stars that fall;
a lost galaxy of nurture with our mother's milk;
a miracle we make it here without a hitch.
This buzzing hive of life, this golden bounty,
honey of survival in our ancestors' sweat,
salt tears for those who don't survive the quickening.

to Melpomene — Muse of Tragedy

Of Odysseys and Other Rambles

Yap yap! Ráiméis and rigmarole! If these walls could speak:
Hentown blather clucked from threshold to attic room,
fabrications, downright lies, home truths and lullabies.
Story snagged from time, spun into the yarn of the house,
the ghostly racket of the carriers of tales
who lug their water buckets up and down the stairs,
all gossip, all frittery bustle, their epic.

If musing on the ornamental frieze of oak,
an iridescent bird through a canopy of air
lets drop a feather to your hand, then use it as a quill
to enumerate such fates, damned or auspicious;
the census of this shelter might immortalize
such vestige of lives endured through crash, through boom,
flitting like some magpie, stolen trinket in her beak.

to Calliope — Muse of Epic Poetry

Funny Ha Ha And Funny Peculiar

Laughter, they say, is nature's best medicine:
through thick and thin, through paucity and plenty,
with your glass half empty, with your glass half full,
if you have a glass, a pot to piss in, a jam jar,
a fork when it's raining soup, when god slams one door
in your face, then locks the other door and bars the window —
you'd have to laugh, or else you'd break down and cry.

It's hard to take the cosmic joke when kids are hungry,
when the cupboard is bare and the fuel's running low;
sniggers, guffaws, snorts, pratfalls and gallows humour.
Is it funny ha ha or funny peculiar
when one by one neighbours take ill, are listless, eyes dull?
Words like typhoid, diphtheria, rickets and dysentery
wipe the smile off your face, invite terror to creep in.

to Thalia — Muse of Comedy

Our Lady of the Apocalypse

Our Lady of the Apocalypse who never
closed your heart to the dissolute, pray for us
who gave shelter in broken-down Georgian tenements,
who kept the doors open to the demented ones,
those who came in rags and miasmas of foul odour,
in delirium tremens, the worn-out old spunkers,
the displaced relicts of imperial trauma.

O sweet daughter of Memory, veiled in enigma,
who brought longed-for oblivion to the meths drinkers,
the dipsos, the alcos, the put-down no-hopers,
those who came in from chaos, from cold, from winds, from rains,
to sleep it all off in hallways, in stairwells, who rent
the long night with sobs, who cried out to you in the throes
of their last agony, grant them eternal succour.

to Polyhymnia — Muse of Sacred Poetry

Envoi

The Daughters of Memory

They're hanging out the sheets on the lines
to catch a spring wind. The children dream
of schooners under a cloud of sail
and the ghosts are packing up their satchels.

They know it's time to leave, with the tide
of history ebbing through the house.

Go you too, mortal, your fated road.
May fixed stars guide you, until you reach
safe harbour, a place you can call home.

For the Hungry Ghosts

At the Sign of the White Horse

We called it a day; we called it a night.
There was absinthe; there was tsipuro.
There was amnesia; there was oblivion.
The waves far out were wild and white capped
But those close in lapped and lipped at the shore

Like whispers, like kisses.
A red-sailed schooner made in for safe haven.
The barman's arms were tattooed with skulls,
And crosses like kisses round his neck were a rosary.
Or a garrotte. I remember thinking. If thinking it was.

I was three sheets to the wind and listing to starboard.
So I offer this witness with caveat and warning.
The children played on the sand — their squabbles microcosmic
To the storm that was brewing. Chair toppling squalls blew
My lines off my sheet, my sheets off the lines.

So much to remember; so much to forget.
The sun was setting; a new moon rising.
It was sextile Neptune, if it matters to you.
It matters to me, my first day sober.
I died in your arms at the sign of the white horse.

My old self tucked in a bed of soft clay
In that port of white towers, white houses, white streets.
The leaves that dropped on my grave were blessings;
The white rose you laid there a token of hope.
The winter would shrive me, would scour me, would save me.

When I rose from the dead I was dressed in white linen.
My angel of mercy, my angel of kindness,
Wreathed in myrtle, smelling of pine.

On your milk-white steed with your milk-white promises:

I was lady
    of as much land
        as I could ride in a long summer's day.

Runes

Who loved the cards
And the cocaine spoon
Who loved the coins

The bronze bowl filled with ink
Who climbed the cliff
Who surfed the katabatic wind

Down down down —
Old friend, my nemesis
Ghost in my mirror

Wreathed in my breath
Shadowing my every move
I will never be free of you

Who never grew old
I plait my long grey hair
I am karyatid to you

The weight of your world on my head

After rain, wind
And the ash tree shakes down droplets
Asperges me, Domine, hyssopo et mundabor

Nine swans glide with the river
They will not carry your soul away
Ghost in my mirror, old friend

When we cut you down
When we laid you out —
Your golden curls, your slippered feet

We washed you, we dressed you
In velvet and silk.

And what of the words you left behind?
Spidery marks in a child's jotter?

File under mystery
File under misunderstood.

Little Addict

'I can't even remember what it was I came here to get away from'
—Bob Dylan

Trails behind me
Through the field of poppies
Their suffragette colours
Green leaves, purple petals
Promise of dream
And end of all pain

Little spite girl
Nails unsheathed
Spitting venom
Your colossal bitterness
How you love the rack
The Catherine Wheel

You have me worn out
Chatter chatter chatter
Dogging my footsteps
Sniffing my heels
I thought you were done for
But you're not done with me

Little sleeveen whinger
Little Sphinx, you have bound me
Jinxed me, even the bees
Smell it, even the cows
In their clover meadow
The goats on the mountain

Even my own tawny she-owl and
Every other wingèd being knows it
Pity me, you say
And you are pitiless
On your ordained line
Down the death track

I have wasted my life —
Wildflowers, moons, the gates of awe
Little addict, dear mercurial mirror
My own private alter-life there
In your narcotic pupils
Regarding nothing, not a thing

I was done with you but
You were not done with me
And here you are
As large as life and twice as ugly
Beside me on the beach
The sea's strong suck

Drowns out your whine
Wave after wave crashing
To the shore hour after hour
As the tourists leave
And the village closes down
For the winter that must surely follow

Soon now — only me and little addict
And the storm front further south
That we know by the swell
White horses, hoof taps on the shingle
In suck — out suck
In time with my breathing

But little addict fidget
Spinning your wheel beside me
Of fortune, of fame
The luck of the draw
Little hip gunslinger
Little eiron of the last laugh

This side of damnation
I have never been so low
And you, you have never been so high
With your warped wheel
Lumbering over the mudflats
Bockety in the ruts

Little evangelist for the dark
You're a model for it
The smell of devil off of you
The whiff of sulphur
You were born for it
Hell, you were born to it

Hawks hang off the mountain
What have they spotted far below?
Little mouse — run! hide!
I watch the ants processional
Purposeful on their path
From underground citadel

To a crust of bread
All day they are at it, all fucking day
Their supply chain, their chain gang
Intent lines of consciousness
Look! One crosses my page
Lumbering over

My inked and scored-out lines
My pied mirror, my angelic sheets
Reflecting your broken mouth
Your sharp little teeth
Your perfectly formed skull
And every random thought it might contain

The ferry crosses the horizon line
And soon … now … now … now
The backwash comes crashing into the bay
A froth of spume left strewn on the shore
I do not think
The ferry comes for me

Let me sleep at last little addict
Here in the salty wash of sea
Here in sinking sun
Here in rising moon
Let me waste my life, little addict
Breath by marvellous breath

The Scales

It is not my story;
Though it set my body resonating.
Memories came flooding into mind

The way it flowed from her —
And we hardly met,
Randomly next to each other on the beach.

I didn't even know her name.
We'd been swimming. We were huddled in towels.
The children floated on plastic rings.

The village was end-of-season melancholic:
Closing up — closing down
For the winter.

And of what would we speak
But the Civil War — an oxymoron —
Here on this prison island:

How communists, labour leaders, artists,
The intelligentsia, a radical generation
Were posted on the local poor,

Delivered by boat and left, it would seem,
To their own devices, a leavening
Still katabolic nearly eighty years after.

⌒

My father, he was captured.
He was to be shot.
My grandfather, he was a rich man.

Not very rich, you understand,
But he could borrow. He had land.
He had houses. My grandmother had jewels.

The fascists came with a scales.
In one pan they placed my father.
My grandfather filled the other pan with gold.

He bought my father's life.
After the story always ends:
'He was worth his weight in gold.'

A small boat putters off towards Fourni
Writ on my English map as 'Ovens'.
They say pirate gold is buried there

That island of myriad coves,
The straits between us a graveyard of shipping wrecks,
Of drowned men in their chains, of fabled cargoes.

There's Patmos too of the Revelator,
Of ancient mushroom cultic frenzy,
Called here 'Boat of Stone'

And Samos of the refugees in their camps,
War-displaced from Syria and Afghanistan,
And beyond again the coast of Turkey,

Ghost ships from Athens heading for Troy
Passing these islands that come and go in the haze.

⁀

My grandfather bought my father's life
But not his liberty.
He suffered the war in a camp in the north.

He joked he'd have only cost half his price
If they'd waited ..... I am sorry.
It is funny in my language.

⁀

But she is weeping and there is nothing to be said.
It is not my story.
I may not even have the right to record it.

But I believe it was prompted
By the dream I carried from last night:
A red-winged angel with a trumpet of gold

Sounding reveille to the resurrected souls
Restored to their young bodies,
Naked in an apocalyptic dreamscape

So that when she spoke it was as if
Our dead rose around us
Their sad flags unfurling, their battle hymns, their slogans,

Lost in what a father must do
To save a son.

At Wattie Meehan's Funeral

Because I believe if you save one person
you save the whole world, I honour the man
who came up to me at my grandfather's funeral.
The way he was twisting his cap, a shy man I saw,
afraid of intrusion. Or offending.
Afraid of the wrong word, at the wrong time:
I know it well. Foot in mouth. Bad call.
The churchyard was thronged with mourners,
a noisy mill on a sunny day, and we were happy
that Wattie had had a last cigarette, a last cup of tea,
had gone to sleep and never woken up. If you
have to go, there are worse ways of leaving.

'Are you the poet? I think you should hear this:

When I was a child, young, five, maybe six,
I was in the Lock Hospital with my mother.
She was dying and I was sick with the fever.
I had it bad. I'd say I was a goner. Sure nobody
came out of there alive. Every pox. Rampant.
A lot of the old Monto whores ended up there.
I think I was written off. I had no one.

Wattie came in. He picked me up,
threw me over his shoulder, carried me
across the river and home to Hannah
there on Railway Street. He laid me down on a blanket,
told Hannah to nurse me. That she did.
Out of the fever, back to life. Look at me.
I'm nearly sixty. I've kids of my own.
Grandkids. They gave me that: Wattie. Hannah.
He'd a great heart, but he'd never let on.
What do you think of that now?'

Hannah, my grandmother, a young mother then,
in the tenement room where satyrs chased nereids
around the stuccoed ceiling, while her babies
bawled & crawled, and sometimes, so she told me,
crumbling plaster shook down like snow —
that I turn here into a blessing from the otherworld,
on my grandfather kneeling at the hearth,
rolling up old newspapers. He ties them in knots,
chops wood for kindling, one eye on the child.
The room is a madding dance, that ironic acoustic
I've spent my whole life constructing again
and again from hints and clues and only half-said things.

I Open the World Like a Box of Colours

The tin box of childhood, of Christmas, of birthdays,
The pristine tiles in rows, the lid a palette,
The brush dipped & pointed & loaded
And the day a fresh sheet waiting
For the wash, the mark, the line;
And as I work I stand in memory,

In solidarity with my dying father
Who brought home stiff white paper
From the racetrack, from his arcane job:
A *bookmaker's clerk* — what might that be?
It was all mystery to me in my girlhood, in the 1960s.
I thought he made books, those wingèd angels,
My heart's delight flapping through those lost rooms,
The tenements, the rentals, the illegal lets.

I told him all this not long before he died;
How the purloined paper where he scanned
Out the names and the horses' odds, evens, the prices,
Presaged what my life would become,
A maker of books, a maker of marks on the page,
How patterns emerge, distort, resume,
How the dúchas briseann trí shúile an chait,
How all the puzzling crosswords,
All the horses' names, the greyhounds, their lineages,
The narratives the bookies and the punters called *form*

Were part now of my own molecular spin,
My drift of years not random, but determined,
Willed by these charms of fate
These whorls in the flux of our journeys.
And if he made sense of what I was saying,

Or of what I was trying to say, he never let on.
Taciturn to the end, he kept his counsel.

We were standing at his door in Mellowes Court
Waiting for the downpour to abate
Regarding an old snuffling very melancholy
Border collie with matted fur, one eye blue, one brown,
A dreadlocked spectre at the gates of time.
Both of us nearing the end of our roads, he said.

The rain stopped and the world, even in the face
Of his dying, was new-minted and fresh.
The suburban murmuration at the end of summer,
Bumblebees and strimmers, resumed.
Too many of your friends died young, he said.
The sad fucking losers, the sad fucking winners ...

We shuffled up to Finglas village for a pint
And a carvery lunch in the Shamrock,
A bet in Paddy Powers, a fiver each way
On Nick-Nick, offspring of Mrs. Santa and Satan
Which he noticed, as I knew he would,
The sire and the mare had anagrammed each other,
A fact that pleased us both greatly & equally
Though the horse lost the race by five lengths
And this poem took a decade and more to make.

I open the world like a box of new colours
Each morning pristine, full of promise,
And there's my father, and all my belovèd dead
Holy icons in the chapel where I go
To light candles for their peace and for mine,
Before I close the lid on the world
That winks out with the wheeling stars above.

The Outcome

The way she read the X-ray
Put me in mind of Madame S
That time in Bundoran —

The purse of her lips, her narrowed eyes,
The way she nodded her head
Confirming her worst fears —

She didn't have to say anything.
The imagery spoke for itself:
The high tower, the lightning strike,

The flames from the window
The couple falling head-first from the heights
And all the blackness of night

To frame the chaos. Things fall apart.
What Madame S said: Do not resist change
Or the Universe will force it on you.

And all the words that trawled in the wake —
Upheaval, cataclysm, destruction, loss,
Revolution, extreme endings, annihilation.

The Tower may fall but the hand
Must still be played whether or not
There is anything worth losing.

Or saving. And so I say, bring it on,
Let fall what will fall.
I'll take the time left,

I'll pull the plug on the machine,
Its tyranny, thief of my days.
I'll go back to the old tools,

This pen, this notebook,
The practice between me and the page
Sufficient unto the day

I lie back in a summer meadow
To permit the smouldering ruins
Settle into their peace.

Last night the owl

Summoned me from a dream
Ke-wick ke-wick ke-wick —

The female tawny owl who flitted
From tamarisk to mastic

For hours — *ke-wick ke-wick ke-wick* —
Till I rose and without stopping for my clothes

Stepped out into the night. The moon
Was void-of-course and the landscape

I walked out into was the very dreamscape
I'd woken out of, to her calls. I followed her

To a jade-green pool. Poppies, windflowers,
Among the grasses. The Plough was overhead

And one star shone golden in the jade-green sky.
Ke-wick ke-wick ke-wick —

I understood as *Quick! Quick! Quick!*
But I could not catch sight of her.

I knelt by the pool, I waded in, I scooped
The jade-green water over my head, my neck.

I understood this as absolution for all transgression
But to whom offered, or for what offered

I cannot tell. My own reflection
Rippled on the water and of a sudden

The owl was mirrored from the depths.
I heard the he-owl call from deeper in the woods —

To-who to-who to-who.
Dawn was breaking over the island,

Our own familiar local star rising
When I slipped quietly into the house.

My lover sleeping in the fret of tangled sheets
Would never know my dream, the world it conjured for me

Nor the night's ritual, nor the owl's counsel,
Her urgency, her fluency, her mystery.

Sun Bath

The linguist who washed up beside me on the beach
Tells me *sunne* in Old English was feminine,
Something I'd intuited long ago in class:
I tested Mother Sun, Sister Sun on my tongue
And saw her ride a white horse across the heavens,
Her corona a wreath of sunflowers round her head.

And brought home, lying there, that everything in reach,
The linguist, the gull, the sandfly, oestrogen,
Adrenaline, melanin, breath itself that passed
Through my ageing body was her immortal song.
I drowsed in the fret of my petty obsessions
Tracking a mote on the inside of my eyelid,

A fleck of colour — intense cerulean blue,
Surrounded by a nimbus of emerald green
Like a planet wandering against the fixed stars.
If there is any consolation to be found
In the place I go where light can barely reach me
Where I hold on by my fingertips to this life,

It is our absolute dependence on our true
Mother: how she offers a sense of proportion;
How in the future, in five or so billion years
Her work will be done with this earth, the very ground
Of our being, of memory, of prophecy.
Mercury, Venus, our own blue planet engulfed,

Consumed in our glorious Mother's death throes —
A redemptive perspective as that ant mooches
Across my sketchbook, across my light-addled lines.

The Lionhearted

Sometimes, she said, with massage things come up.
Your tears do not worry me. Stuff lodges
In the body. Feel free. To weep. To shed.

Like a snake its skin; like a crab its shell.
The tears run down my face into my ears.
I am stretched, a starfish on a blue sheet

Under the shade of the tamarisk trees,
The surf pounds the rocks below, cicadas
Are bowing their tune again and again.

Again. Chrysacheira above me
Pressing on my limbs with her palms
Pressing, pawing like a big red cat.

Suddenly my mother, emissary
Of the underworld, a great big red cat,
Her paws kneading my child body, my paws

Kneading her breasts, nuzzling towards her nipple
Hungry mouth searching through the stink of her,
The fog of nicotine that wreaths her head.

She — a big red cat; I — a small grey mouse.
Timid inside the wardrobe, hiding from her rages,
Her grief, the belt with the silver buckle.

I'll beat that accent out of you. Common.
Common as muck. You little guttersnipe.
Big red cat with her sharp claws unsheathed.

There is a place inside of me where you
Are always walking up the avenue.
I see you from the front seat of the bus.

I am heading into college. I'm late
For a lecture: The Origins of Myth.
Some lessons I will have to learn over and over again.

I should have quit the bus, I should have run to you
And taken the heavy bags from your hands,
I should have smoothed your cramped and blistered hands

Finger by swollen finger, I should have stood
Shoulder to shoulder with you, I should have walked
The road with you — even into hell.

Seventy-seven and then some lightyears
Away — I place you now, beloved mother,
In your own starry constellation fixed

Between Virgo to the east and Cancer
To the west, crouching over the sun this
Peaceful morning like a cat with your ball

Of light. I will raise my face to you, lion
In your cave of dreams; I will stand my ground:
Herculean mouse, my first labour done.

Ends & Means

It is the old argument
In the *cafeneion*
Fuelled by *tsipuro*, fuelled by impotence,
Fuelled by despair.
I am weary of their armchair revolution
I am weary of their endless talk.
The generation of '68, the children of longing.

They are old now in the thermal springs
With the young hypochondriacs
The post-plague beau monde.
They sit in the pool the villagers have built of stone
To corral the boiling waters where they meet the Aegean Sea.
They are a privileged parliament, a hung jury.
They have come for a cure; they have come for redemption.

Last night I dreamt my children were young.
We walked hand in hand down the meadow
Then single file through the forest gathering mushrooms.
Deeper we went into the dappled light until
Off trail, stumbling over downed trees,
Snagged by undergrowth, sticky with pine resin,
Our clothes torn, our legs scratched, hair messed.

When we emerged into the clearing
My children's hands were become claws,
Their bodies furred, their mouths become snouts.
They faced me at the forest edge and snarled,
My little bears, they turned and left me
To waken, my cheeks wet with tears.

I carry my dream like a holy wound into the day.

The icon's finger points to her heart.

I light two candles for my two lost bears.

In the pool the bodies glisten —
Senescent, nubile, in the radionic waters.

This is an ancient *aesklepion*.
The sick slept in the sanctuary of the site
And waited for a dream.
The therapy
Depended on how the dream was read.

So the classical scholar tells me.

Off island, the forests burn, in Attica, in California, in Siberia,
The news a toxic fog.
The pastoral become radical again;
A poem about a tree to root us –
Blessed be bole, blessed be branch, blessed be leaf,
Blessed be all the tree shelters.

The blessed sequoias — great-grandmothers
Burning ring by ring: bell note of a thousand years
Tolling.

The salt water laps at the edge of the pool.
I am silent in the murmur of voices
The argument has moved on to civil wars.
How many generations for truth to be told?
I do not think there is time enough to heal.

The classical scholar talks of the Fates.
The three robed in white: Clotho, Lachesis, Atropos —
She who spins, she who measures, she who cuts.
It is all talk to me; all moon talk.

I think of my sister in the sweat-shop
Sixteen years old at her machine —
Her apprenticeship begun, her golden hair,
Her shining soul:
She cut the thread of her own life.

The heart wound too much for her.

The waves break on the pebbles,
Lace on the petticoat of the great mother.

I walk in sunlight along the ridge.
I pick hawthorn berries to make a tincture
To strengthen the heart.

Eight minutes for the sun's light to reach me.
Four million tons of matter into energy every second.

This I believe.

The Lovers

In the room next door: all night
their weeping and wailing.
This morning in the merciless heat
They are sullen, they are silent,
At breakfast separate tables.
He faces the sea.
She faces the mountain.

It is what we have named *The Piraeus Syndrome* —
Dawn at the ancient port of Athens
Where the ships set sail for Troy.
Neither of us can remember now
What the row was about.
I hoisted my backpack, you hoisted yours;
We headed for different ferries.

That might have been that —
Another fling, the passion burned off,
The world an ashen waste.
I would lick my wounds,
You would lick your wounds.
We were young and resilient
Though we did not know that then.

I thought my fire would destroy me,
Would destroy all I turned my hand to.
What prompted us in the noise and bustle
The morning work of the port,
To look back and find each other again?
Through the milling crowds
The spark glanced, arced

And caught us in its kindling.
I want to approach them:
I want to say be patient, be kind,
Or not impatient, or not unkind
To each other, to each's others —
Those hovering ghosts that trail us
Across the face of the earth.

Shades of history, they speak through us,
They make weapons of our tongues.
They are jealous of our beauty
Our beating hearts, oh hungry ghosts.
My grandmother says they come
When our guardian angels are sleeping.
I want to show the breaking lovers

The gift you bought me that morning
We nearly threw our fate to the wind,
After yoghurt and honey and
The sweet kisses of our peace —
Aphrodite's charm, a golden egg
Inlaid with bands of blue enamel
As blue as the sky this morning.

I want to tell the breaking lovers
That while they screamed their pain
The equinox moon outside,
Full in the sign of Virgo
Jupiter and Venus to her right
The Little Bear, his Mother,
And all the heavenly creatures

Wheeling overhead continued
Reciting their ancient stories over and over.
For what else can they do?

I want to tell them that thirty years on
We have not regretted cutting through
The chaos of that morning
To find each other again,

Though that of itself guaranteed nothing —
It was not the end, not by a long shot,
Of our loneliness when we stood
Hand in hand at the water's edge
And gazed together into the merciful eternal.

Watching the ferries come & go

'cursed is the ground for thy sake:
in sorrow shalt thou eat of it all the days of thy life'
— Genesis 3:17

Watching the passengers wash off
Watching the passengers wash on

And the clamour of cars, vans, motorbikes,
The lorries with ΜΕΤΑΦΟΡΕΣ

Written on their side, shifting goods to and from
The island, the charm of that word for a poet,

Metaphors being our stock in trade
And are ΜΕΤΑΦΟΡΑΚΙ little carriers? Those vans?

The coming and going of souls
Has all my attention now.

It's coffee in the sunshine, online news from home:
Funerals, plague statistics, metadata, gossip,

Deliriums and rumours, folklore
Of the variants, the pro-vaxers, the anti-vax gangs

That wash in and out of mind.
And here's another ferry docking and the backwash as it docks

That bobs the local craft in the harbour up and down
And the klaxons and alarms start up all over again.

We watch the latest refugees,
Patient in their razor-wired compound, we watch

The holiday-makers the town's merchants,
The wheelers and the dealers,

The students and the soldiers and the guards.
The young one who catches my eye —

She's pregnant, near her time, in a white gown
Patterned with roses. She's hot and bothered by flies.

She is altogether beautiful; like a figure
From out the archaic, from a frieze —

Emblem of fecundity, the world's deep longing to renew.
Such are my thoughts when the painter nearby

Starts holding forth in a very loud voice.
She has caught his eye too. He would paint her

Seated on a cushioned chair. Red to amplify
The colour of the flowers on her dress. A throne.

She deserves a throne. As if she were an empress
On whose lands the sun never set.

He would paint her by water. Flowing water.
He would crown her with a tiara of stars.

A laurel wreath. A sheaf of wheat. Pearls.
An orb. She is majestic, he says. An earth goddess!

Stop: stop: stop: I cannot bear it.
I am ashamed of myself.

So little between us in our venal imaginings.
She regards us from behind the razor wire

Corralled there with those others for the camp.
She pities us. Our aged bodies. Our failing sight.

The klaxon sounds and the crowd surges forward,
They shuffle up the gangplank into the maw of the ship.

One day soon the ferry will come for us,
My love, we will walk away from this place

And the life we have made, hand in hand,
Away from its nourishment, our stories.

I once thought of Adam and Eve cast out of Paradise
As part of a creation myth, refined

To serve an imperial mindset, a version
To be resisted in the struggle for sanity.

I understand it now as prophecy, and this
The last chapter, the last verse: as if we

Had eaten too little, too late, of the knowledge
Of our own ignorance, our own unbecoming.

Hymn to the Bat

Eleni says:

'The young men go up there to get bat wings.'
A mysterious utterance that begs
The question: 'For what do they need bat wings?'
'A bat wing in the trouser pocket makes
The man irresistible to women.
It increases the desire for the bed.'
Eleni likes to wind me up with story,
To reel me in and land me like a fish,
And I'm a willing lubber on her line,
All ears for clues to what makes this place tick.

Of course, I Google *aphrodisiacs*
+ *bats* and lose myself in their dark realm
An hour or more — their high testosterone,
Their gland secretions mixed with their urine
To attract and hold a mate. No stranger
Than our own peculiar mating urges
If we grant them parity of esteem,
Dear flittermice, dear leather flappers, dear
Lucifugous creatures of my dreamtime
Fly-by-nights who stitch land to sea to sky.
And remarkably (I remark) there is no truth
To the saying *as blind as a bat:* keen-eyed,
Keen-eared, tuned to low light conditions.

⤴

I had come on it at dusk — the old mine.
Abandoned now, its tunnel like a mouth

Into the very pit of hell itself,
Puffing out hot air in rhythmic patterns
From deeper in the belly of the earth
As if a dragon be imprisoned there
And though the sun had set, a sapphire glow
Was in the sky, Jupiter and Venus
Already brightening above the mountain.

I meant to enter only as far as
Light allowed. Thirty feet in I was stopped
In my tracks: Did I disturb the colony?
Or were they heading out as usual
To hunt in the gloaming? I stood dead still.
They came onto me — a cloud, a *cauldron*
Of seething darkness. Not a wing touched me,
As they passed with their keen eyes, their keen ears,
A rippling river that flowed around me.

I felt their passage as a blessing, their breeze
A fellow-creaturely kiss on my skin
That seemed to open me and allow night enter
And take possession of my soul
Leaving me emptied, fearless, and alone.

The Key

Dear world: what you bring me each morning
In the bowl of quietness our lives have become —
Old grief, old sorrow in a new poem.

❧

Looking across the straits at Samos
And beyond that island to Turkey,
Thinking of Yannis Ritsos, I spin
The lines from his diaries of exile
From the sodden prison rooms
Where he wrote on scraps of paper
On opened-out cigarette packets
Where he brought his great-hearted compassionate gaze
To the young soldiers who guarded him
When at dawn they rubbed the dream from their sleepy eyes.
Where he tracked the black cat across the camp
Under the light of the moon in her phases,

Where memory was a basket of lemons
And a woman plaiting her hair in a garden
He dreamt the shuttered windows of his abandoned house
Were opened, the lamps lit, the bread cooling on the sill
A young man singing rembetika
While the stew simmers and the table is set
For the guests who would come
With bouzouki and guitars and poems in their pockets.

❧

A young woman, I hitchhiked the length of Europe
To find what his poems promised:
The mountain path that winds down to the sea
And the cool of the village fountain,
Men at games of chess, cats napping on the sill,
A woman sitting in her doorway
Who had once fought in the mountains,
Embroidering some daughter's dowry.

I carried those poems like lanterns
Against the darkness of my own country;
I carried them like my own truth
To consider my own history in the brutal light of the south.

I was too young to know what the state erases,
What it does to poets who will not forswear their comrades,
Who will not sign the papers of renunciation.

In my own city at a workshop, just before the plague
Had driven us to our screens, had chained us to our machines,
There was a refugee: we were speaking of trauma
And where it lodges in the body. Look,
She said, this is all I carry from my old life.
It was a brass key, ordinary, like my own house key.
She wore it around her neck, strung on a red leather thong.
I imagined her returning to her bombed and wounded city,
Picking through the rubble of the street to her old front door,
And nearly said this aloud but was stopped by a look
As if she had read my mind: No, there is nothing there,
The house, the tree, the street, my only daughter,
My two sons, the blue door that the key once opened.

Little Moons

Was what she called the white pills
That took her far away from us in those days.
Thrown down on a blue tablecloth — little moons.

And as the nights waxed and waned, they worked
Or they didn't. She would or she wouldn't
Stick around. She would or she wouldn't

Take a blade to the delicate skin
Of her beautiful arms that I remember
Weaving over her head as she danced at sixteen

In a dress of green velvet. And sometimes
She was wired directly to the moon. I'd walk
Beside her, holding her hand

As if she might take off at any moment.
You are all that tethers me to the earth,
She said, a week before she left for good.

Nights sometimes I walk and wonder
Where she is or went, nights I cannot sleep,
The moon snagged in the pines,

The estuary waters still and mist
Seeping in from the sea till I am veiled
And grey like a revenant myself.

She loved the beach, the coves, the cliff path,
The whole scape, land and water,
Every fox, owl, bat, every nook & cranny,

And the day creatures too, the moons by day.
But most, she loved her little moons
Flung down, a dare, on a blue tablecloth.

She opened the night like a door to me,
Its earthshine & starlight, its furnace of desire,
Her head bent in devotion, the slick of her body

As she danced was a seal in the harbour
After.
       And that last day we sat watching
A mother crow teach her two fledglings

To soften hard crusts of bread, to drop them
Into the dog's waterbowl, to bob them
With their beaks till they were soaked right through.

I remember her laughter. I remember thinking
These simplicities might save her. If the world
Could slow enough for her attention

To fashion some cord of attachment.
If she could open to the divers tongues
Of the creatures she loved, their songs. My song.

But she had no attachment except to the moons
That bound her, little moons
Laid down on a blue tablecloth.

Surprised by Joy, I Turned

in sleep and woke to a February morning
carrying the dream recurrent
all that second winter of the plague —

a chariot made of ice or so I surmised
ornate and radiant
in the dream sunlight.

I reached my hand to touch
expecting to blast my fingers
the way what is cold

can feel like fire.
My hand was wet: the chariot
was made of water

held together by an act of my own will.
I understood.
It was intention that kept the molecules spinning

in their proper order,
the absolute attention of my dreaming self.
Every night I dreamt that dream

I expected ice, found water,
and every night I kept the transport
fit for purpose,

the journey into the new morning
carrying its cargo of joy,
its rags of light

home to you, my beauty,
to the morning's cloud herding,
to the dishevelled dawn.

Of Knives and Other
Unfinished Lockdown Business

Faffing about the house in search of my Opinel
the one from the island, a favoured tool, its honed edge,
its haft of olive wood, its snug, smooth fit to my hand,
always close with my pen, my notebook, in backpack or
pocket, as I ramble, as I rove out the days of my life.

The way, as happens, a thing becomes more than itself,
becomes crucial, obsessional, grows to essential
so that everything stops, the house upside down,
life, luck, law and liberty bound in its meaning, no work
to be furthered until it's found. Hierophantic!

Vital to my ordinal daily grind, my lost knife.
Saint Anthony deaf to me; discombobulated;
possibly, if examined too closely, pathological,
this rage for order of a certain kind — being a patterner
by trade, be the pattern discerned with ease or with struggle.

To distract myself and to rescue the write-off that was the morning,
I hang out the sheets on the line to catch the winds –
dream sails white against the azure sky of eternity.
Heraldic in memory: another island,
another knife, a gift of a dying friend, long ago

when the world was young to me and I was finding my way.
Hand forged of carbon steel, the haft inset with ivory,
the crux gemina, the patriarchal cross. When I wrapped
my hand about it, I felt the intent in its form:
one day it would be used to wound, to maim, to kill.

I am fanciful by nature, but such was the tug,
the shift of tides, the undertow, that I quit my job
and travelled on foot across the White Mountains
to the Asklepion of Lissos, to the sacred spring,
and washed it and dried it and buried it deep in the roots

of an ancient olive, for it was not my fate to destroy it
or its fate to be destroyed.
                        And what of the Opinel? Its fate?
I ransacked the sheds, I hoked through the bins. You found it
weeks later in a gardening jacket like a blessing
bestowed on the simple, grounded, nature of this life.

Of Wrens and Other Singers

After the dementia ward
Where we sat in the sunroom
Under the sign *Tir na nÓg*
(Mercy or sarcasm, we wondered?),

After the examinations,
The estimations, the calibrations,
Of mind, of memory, of recall,
We sat in innocence, in peace,
Your hand in mine,

Waiting for what the tests might tell.
The other patients came and went,
The rain tattooed its news upon the roof —
News of forest & mountain & the angry sea.
The wind that shook the panes was a voice
Keening our lost childhood.

I left you then, swaddled in tartan,
A goodbye kiss soft as a feather.

That morning pottering about the garden
I'd come upon a wren's nest
With a clutch of speckled eggs
Abandoned in the mouth-hole
Of a whitewashed wooden mask —
I'd hung it up to spook intruders
Should they brave the back wall
Believing as I do that fear
Is easily bred by triggering
The iconography of our earliest days.

The nest — a thing of beauty,
Wrought of dog hair & down & straw,
Lichen & crisp curled leaves &
Filaments of black plastic netting
And the vivid green moss
Like humpety velvet cushions.

I had seen the nesting pair
About the place for weeks
Their trills, their bustle,
Their hoppity company as I dug my drills,
And early one freezing morning
I saw the very breath of the male
As he sang, as he sang, as he sang.

I do not know where their story ended —
A magpie or other wingèd ravager?
Sooty McQuillan on his night patrols? —
Or why their abandoned nest
Should grieve me so: it must be
The way that we transfer pain
From great unbearable loss
To something manageable at least,
From the lost cosmos that is one human mind
To a wren's breath of a frosty morning.

The Poet's Funeral Mass

The webcam shows the altar, the first rows of pews
at the front of the church. Still empty.
The sacristan hovers into view, taps the mic,
moves deftly about at the details of vessels,
of linens, of the Holy Book, tweaks the flowers.

Out there in the parish, I picture the neighbours
ranged along the kerbside as the hearse passes,
the applause rippling around the cortege.

I fancy the very land herself grieves,
the tumultuous rivers, the streams haring
down the mountainside, the suburban streets;
and in the city along the deserted
thoroughfares, the statues with their blind eyes
their stony robes, their indifferent repose.

We wait drinking tea in the kitchen, bread
cooling on a wire rack, an abandoned draft,
the dog with his head in my lap, the way he knows
something is wrong, that the masters are sad.

Outside in the spring sunshine, hyacinths
and those asphodels we brought back as bulbs
from the Gorge of the Dead at Kato Zakros
have pushed through their mulch of leaf litter,
hungry for the light of this world, its flowering.

Last night, Eavan, I dreamt I saw your face, (like Athena's
on the shield of Achilles) in a bronze bowl
filled to the brim with ink, the scrying bowl
of Nostradamus, herbalist, plague doctor,

poet. In his attic room above Paris.
He was there beside me, his hand on my shoulder
wearing his beaked plague mask, herb stuffed,
the waxed canvas gown, the leather caul,
the eyeholes of sugar-glass to protect his eyes.
He smelt of oregano, the mountains of the south.

In dream you talk of his macaronic verses,
of how he has been in print for over
five hundred years, of the human hunger
for prophecy, the gulf between what the maker
means and what the reader makes of it.
And of how tired you are of the journey.

All this flits like sunlight over the garden
through my mind in the minutes before the requiem
begins in the grainy monotone livestream.
The permitted ten mourners, your closest,
your dearest, follow your coffin, settle
to the ceremony. I think you would
appreciate the stark and simple truth
of the matter, you who disdained ornament
and distrusted rhetoric, the venal pomp.

Though sundered from the comfort of each other
in kitchens, in offices, in studies, in dorm rooms,
in cabins plain and houses grandiose
across the face of the earth, her moody oceans,
we mourn you. If we say dignity, love,
silence, longing …. finger the words like obols,
the fare to the other side …. we will also say honour,
gratitude, and bow with the communion bell
to the loneliness we feel at your leaving.

The Grief of Creatures

The old horse comes as usual to the fence
to be fed by the man who leaves the house
in the breaking light of dawn with a sack of early apples.
The mare comes after, and her foal,
like a shy girl at her flank, coming down
the mountainy field through the summer mist.

The rain-drenched stallion in the lower field
pricks up his ears, his companion donkey
patient at the gate. And, oh, they'll be waiting
for the man as he whistles the two dogs to heel
and turns to the wide-open sea where his name
is writ on water. They'll be waiting

the long hours for the man to finish the line
and set down his poem and pick up the bucket
of sweet early apples and climb up the hill to the gate.
They'll be waiting and wondering. Has he fallen
asleep in his bed of nettles, or is he lost
in a mineshaft's coppery dark? They've not

seen him take the boat out the harbour mouth.
They've not seen him step the mast.
But they've smelled a wind off the Atlantic,
the last wind to fill his sails.
The old horse comes as usual to the fence
to be fed, and the mare and her shy foal.

They are waiting for John O'Leary.
He could nearly stretch his hand across the void
to touch the grieving horses,
to stroke their velvet muzzles,
his hands smelling of apples, of salt.

Elegy for Young Love

I

So we were looping in the Ferryman,
drinking ourselves down all that afternoon
and the tunes were looping too round our rapt heads,
through the drunks and vagabonds, like tendrils
pushing, seeking out a purchase on our souls,
the drone bellowing breath as if the piper played us.

Stricken by love, fate, your black narcotic eyes,
the microdots we dropped the night before
the morning after that had landed us here
on the leatherette banquette drinking cider,
apple-mouthed and lost in each other's arms.
If I say weaving it was only the way that
the piper's elbow moved brought to mind warp,
brought to mind weft and swaddling clothes. Or shrouds.

We fell out of there and up the quays in the drizzle.
Everything thereabouts was grey of a sudden:
the granite pavers, the quay walls, the sheets
of sea mist sifting up-river. And the old guy
who tailed us: greyfaced, greysuited, greyeyed
I fancied, and fancied he was a shade,
a grey revenant swathed in a cobweb caul
dogging our steps to the ferry, the way
the city ghosts would manifest and hang
for a while before they latched onto some
other open-hearted passing soul.
I figured he was hungry for the warmth
of the living, for the heat we kindled.

And so he followed us down the steps and climbed
into the boat. He brought his own chill
to the river chill. I felt his dead hand
on my psyche, his eft fingers probing
for a hold on my tripped out dreaming self.
The way the dead do, given half a chance.
I saw them everywhere, all the time.

And what did I say to you, my young love,
on that ebbtide across the river, your eyes
black pools of devotion, so smitten we were?
Nothing. Tongue tied. As was my habit.
Though the dead stalked us and were within
a hair's breadth of your curly head, I said nothing.

II

That was nearly fifty years ago. Imagine.
We'd a cheap winter let in a seaside town,
between the harbour and the beach,
a draughty bungalow with dodgy wiring.
No money much, no television. If I look
down the years to those rooms, there's a chessboard,
a Spanish guitar, there are poems and plays
and a window over our bed casting sealight.
You read me *Ulysses* night after broken night.

Technically we were students. I would
just about get up and take the train to town
but only for those things that turned me on:
WB Stanford's lectures on *The Odyssey*,
the ancient poets and their tragedies.
I was homesick already for Athens.
I wanted to bring you to the islands,

to the white, shining cities of the south,
to find the dinnseanchas of the Bronze Age,
the myths I intuited I might live by.

III

I should have seen which way the wind was blowing,
that year of the Dublin bombings, those bombs
we missed blundering into, by minutes,
rushing from College to the train, the buses
on strike, our story nearly over. That phase.
I nearly died of love in that house by the sea;
while my mother elsewhere was turning her face
to the wall rehearsing her early death. Exeunt all.

I learned heartbreak is a real ache, the heart
battering against the ribs like a creature
tangled in the rigging of a boat. That last storm,
a northerly, kept the trawlers in port,
the house was party after party, the bed
a troubled raft and we poor fools upon it.

IV

I mourn them: our young selves, all the pain
they dished out to each other. And all the years
after, the revenge I took out on so many kind
young men and women who tangled with me.
It was grief and grief only, the grey
cold-fingered reach of it. The hungry ghosts.

This midnight I remember you
in friendship. We survived our wars;

I bow three times in gratitude —
the gifts you gave my young self:
teaching me to play chess the hungry days,
reading me *Ulysses* night after broken night.

Sometimes (I fancy) at a certain conjunction
of the planets, the very taste of our old lives
rises — the very tang and sweetness
of apple in my mouth.

The Hungry Ghosts

There are folk who have skeletons in their cupboards;
I have a warehouse full of them,
stacked to the rafters, my army of the dead.
This be my ossuary: I pick over the bones.

I sift through the ancestors, skull by cluttered
skull, from the burial pits of the archives, item
by scant item. In the chasm secreted
between the folklore and the paper trail, a zone

where truth is hard got, if got at all or ever.
Young I'd wondered where spirit goes when from flesh it severs
and why, in the chambers of my pulsing heart
the music was a mourning song, a dirge, an art

sublime that might have laid the hungry ghosts to rest.
Once after a poetry reading in a midland town
a woman collared me: urgent, earnest
she'd eyes intense, near black, of darkest brown

and this she said: 'Your dead were with you on that stage.
The young dead, the old dead, shades of every age,
babies, crones, toddlers, those in their day the unborn.
I might have unleashed an habitual scorn

of such nonsense, but for a look that flitted across
her face, but for the darkness, but for the light,
but for the grief, I found in her clairvoyant eyes
in a midland town on a winter's night.

And so I listened as the chairs were stacked
and the caretaker swept the aisles,

'They are lonely, they come to hear you; you are wrapped
in their affection; they need your poems, like spells

to unbind them from attachment to our world.'
She turned and left and to this very day I feel
that what she said was a summons, a flag unfurled
in newfound territory, a commonweal

between the here and now, the then and there,
that I might yet come to settle and find peace,
a state of mind, in mind, between the written and the heard
where truth is always tantalising, there — just beyond my reach.

Of Breath, No Breath, & Didgeridoos

All the length of Grafton Street I was played,
the sound resonating in my belly.
I felt it first; then heard it; it lured me
through the crowds, the city noise, the sirens.
It brought me to my knees on the pavement grey.
It filled my every cavity, it thrilled
me to the marrow of my bones. And when
the young aboriginal took a break
he told me he was busking around the world;
he was musician-archeologist by trade.

His story went: once on a dig in his home place
they unearthed an ironwood tube so old
and so long buried it had opalesced.
His the first breath in many a thousand year
to travel the length and enter living ears.
The way he said 'my people' had me close to tears.
I waxed, I waned, I wept, I effervesced.
What was base and toxic turned to gold,
the wonder that breath itself was instrument of grace.

I understood the tune could heal if played
at the body ailing or broken, as it whorled,
as it skirled, as it whirled, to ease ague or ache
or whatever else might ail skin or bone or vein.
These patterned dreamtime cures passed down by skilled
adepts: the right notes in the right, ordered way.
Very like our own pipers coaxing the tunes
from a promise of air, wrested, let free
of the chanter, handwrought and fingered.
                              Oh, tell me,
teach me, show me, where should I offer my gratitude?

Hermitage

My light may be small
And the vastness dark.
But I take to the road.

And where the road ends
I walk the trail blazed
Through the forest long ago

Moving by sightlines — wolf-tree
To wolf-tree through the under-shrubs
And the saplings.

The cabin is still there
By the spring; the quilt
We used sleep under.

I have come to escape
The new Puritans
I have pulled the plug on the machines,

To await the contrarians
When they beat a path to my hearth.
And what do I carry from the city?

The memory of that last day —
My students' boots lined up
In a row at the workshop door

Their backs bent to their poems
Their footprints outside
Vanishing with the snowmelt.

The Walking Cure

In memory of Anna Meehan, nee Plunkett, (1880 – 1933), of Purdon Street, Mabbot Street (now James Joyce Street), and Lower Tyrone Street (now Railway Street), Dublin 1.

And so
I pull myself together and I go

Out the door
My boots waxed and shined, my mind
Besieged by thoughts toxic and unkind

My body
Sore from hunching over books
And all my griefs like rooks at dusk

Come home
To roost

I close the door. I lock it. I throw the key away.

⁓

A TERRIBLE SONNET:

Of course I do not leave my self behind,
Nor my troubling dead who will not let me rest.
My great-grandmother clings to my back, her bony frame
That the wind blows through, I lug along;
The bag of tattered poems my dead friends made
(Who in the world now do I care to impress?);
The file stamped Top Secret from the Republic of Trauma;
And from past lifetimes the residual karma.

Self-disgust, low self-esteem, the distress
Of self-obsession, the self-pity — I wade
Through the psychobabble, the saccharine song,
Every bitter word and every spat out bitter name,
All that demeans me, that brands me less than best —
The path itself will show what needs to be divined.

Spellbind the foot! Bless it!
The forefoot, the midfoot, the hindfoot, bless it.
Its twenty-six bones, its thirty-three joints,
Its more than one hundred ligaments. Bless it!
Bless its arches:
From side to side, from toe to heel, bless its springiness.
Bless the left; Bless the right.

I shoulder my load and hit the road.

After rain the path is tricky,
Fallen slate skids on the bare rock.
The air is resinous after the summer drought

That dried-out lavender, thyme, oregano, sage,
Wild in the mastic maquis. Medicine I inhale the good of.
With every outbreath I let go of pain.

When I climb to the pool
Fed by runoff from the mountain
I unshackle great-grandmother from my back.
How light she has become

In the metrics of my walk.
I sit and take my ease and drink

Of water that is a memory of water
A ghost taste of childhood.
Across the straits, Patmos sails further into the heat haze.

⁀

'And a great portent appeared in heaven, a woman clothed with the sun,
with the moon under her feet, and on her head a crown of twelve stars'
— Revelation 12:1

Snatches of the Book of Revelation come to me;
Of all my childhood hours upon my knees,
In all the glooms of all the Dublin churches and chapels of ease
With the women before the brass candleholders
In the flicker of church light, the murmurings, the clack of beads,
It was Our Lady on the horned moon I loved the best,
The twelve stars about her head, her merciful eyes,
Her radiant palms. Though I would grow to hate the church
And all its corruptions, the child undefiled
Can access still the grace of the love unconditional,
Of my grandmothers, my aunts, in the wash of the choir,
The mesmeric frankincense, their intense devotion,
The women of the parish mopping the aisles.

⁀

Let this be the last haunt of my great-grandmother,
Here beside the pool of clear water
Under the high ridge of the Aetheros,
Where tawny owls call by moonlight.
Let her be water spirit in her element.
Let me not carry her back down the path.

And for the very last time:

I hold her as a fallen leaf on the palm of my hand
Caught in its drift to the ground.

I hold her as a raindrop on the palm of my hand
Beaded mirror to the wounded world.

I hold her as a small pink shell on the palm of my hand
A token the sea cast up on the strand.

I hold her as a robin's blue egg on the palm of my hand
The night's deep mystery remembered in her dark eyes.

Before I turn and head back on the trail
For the cloud-topped summit of the mountain,

I hold her in memory on the palm of my hand
There between my heart line and my life line

Between heaven and earth
Between here and there
Between then and now

For once again, then never again:

Creature most beloved, I return her to the wild.

The Unbecoming

I cast my old self on the funeral pyre;
I cast her tyrannical calendar
After, so all that was base become gold,
Transformed by white heat, by flames furled and whorled.
Pure bell notes carried on the morning air,
My lost innocence restored to their patterned sound —
No longer blest, I was no longer curst.
I faced the void, embraced immensity.

I set out with no maps: I trust the land
Itself to show me the lie of the land.
I travel light, I walk hand in hand with doubt.
It's memento vitae not memento mori
Now. This journey takes all my graft and art,
Featherless plantigrade biped mammal that I am.
I'll measure time by the light of the moon
From forces elemental I'll spin, I'll knit
Comfort blankets for those wounded by my words,
Tongue whipped, scrawbed by my claws, who've felt the blow,
The little dig, the bitter slight, the nasty, the cheap!
Consider the horoscope, not natal, but fatal.
My ravelling or unravelling past
Is ash now, and feeds the flowering thorn.

ACKNOWLEDGEMENTS

Gratitude to Catriona Crowe, Joe Hassett, Kay Foran, Terry Fagan, & Charles Duggan for enlightening conversations; to Pat Boran & Raffaela Tranchino, Dedalus Press; to the many editors, broadcasters, curators who first aired these poems or versions of them.

For The Hungry Ghosts was published in a limited edition by Etym Press, Dublin, 2022, as a response to the Hades episode of James Joyce's *Ulysses* in its centenary year. It was commissioned for *Ulysses 2.2* by ANU Productions, MoLI, and Landmark Productions. It was first presented at The Parade Tower, Kilkenny Arts Festival, 2022, in performance with master piper David Power.

'The Pre-Menstrual Emails', *The Yellow Nib,* ed. Ciaran Carson, Number 4, 2009.

'Seven Stanzas for the Magdalenes', to accompany an exhibition of photographs *After Magdalen* by Ethna O'Regan, Berlin, 2009.

'In Solidarity', *The Stinging Fly,* ed. Declan Meade, Spring, 2009.

'Sufficient Technology', *2x12* for Terence Brown, Occasional Press, Co. Cork, 2010.

'song for the longest night (dig the stillness)', Carols for Christmas, *The Guardian,* 18th December 2010.

'Diamond-Faceted, His Breath', *The Daily Mirror,* 21.03.2011; *Shine On: Irish Writers for Shine,* ed. Pat Boran, Dedalus Press, 2011.

'Ballad of the Fallen World', *Ireland Remembers 9/11,* The Convention Centre Dublin, 2011.

'A Sonnet for Gary Snyder on his 80th Birthday', Cold Mountain Review, ed. Kathryn Kirkpatrick, Spring 2016.

'A Netchke for Barbara Korun', *Southword,* Spring 2011.

'Old Fossil', *What We Found There,* ed. Theo Dorgan, Dedalus Press, 2013.

'The First of February: Howth Head', *This Landscape's Fierce Embrace: The Poetry of Francis Harvey,* ed. Donna L. Potts, Cambridge Scholars Publishing, 2013.

'Gerald Dillon Sonnets', *Lines of Vision: Irish Writers on Art,* ed. Janet McLean, Thames and Hudson, 2014.

'The Solace of Artemis', *20/12: Twenty Irish Poets Respond to Science in Twelve Lines,* Iggy McGovern, Dedalus Press, Dublin 2012; *Notre Dame Review,* Number 34, Summer/Fall, ed William O'Rourke, 2012; *The Guardian: An Anthology of Poems Concerning Global Warming,* ed. Carol Ann Duffy, spoken by Gabriel Byrne, May 2015; *Imaginary Bonnets with Real Bees in Them,* UCD Press, 2016; *Poetry Jukebox,* Paris, curated by Maria McManus & Stephen Sexton, 2019.

'Robin Redbreast', *Christmas Garland,* Candlestick Press, Nottingham, 2016.

'The Artist Regards the Woman Murdered', for the launch of *Women's Aid Report Behind Closed Doors: Femicide Watch 1996–2016.* (incorporated into 'The Walking Cure', p. 155)

'The Merciful Hours', The Irish Hospice Foundation to mark their 30th Anniversary, with Poetry Ireland, 2016.

'Wingéd Woman with Hound', voiced by Ruth Negga, *Talking Statues,* Dublin City Council Project, 2017.

'The Celtic Cross Spread Dictated to Paula Meehan by W.B. Yeats from the Other Side', for a symposium to honour Roy Foster, at the National Library, Dublin, convened by Caitriona Crowe, in 1917.

'Alma Mater', for *Trinity 425 Symposium,* TCD, 2017. 161

'By the Autumn River', *Migrant Shores: Irish, Moroccan and Galician Poetry,* ed. Manuela Palacios, Salmon Poetry, Cliffs of Moher, 2017.

'Young Love', for 'Haiku Wheel' sculpture by Nickie Hayden, Drawing on Joyce, Olivier Cornet Gallery, Dublin 1, 2018. Ulysses Haiku Project, print by Robert Russell, The James Joyce Centre, 2019.

Museum, Paula Meehan & Dragana Jurišić, Dublin City Council Culture Company, Dublin, 2019. 'Museum', *Poetry Ireland Review,* Issue 124, ed. Eavan Boland, Dublin, 2018;

'Sister Trauma', in *The Lea-Green Down,* ed. Eileen Casey, Fiery Arrow Press, Dublin, 2018.

'The Island, A Prospect', in *Shaping Ireland: Landscapes in Irish Art,* ed. Donal Maguire, National Gallery of Ireland, Dublin, 2019.

'At the Spring Equinox' to celebrate the conferral of PhD., Honoris Causa, by Dublin City University on 21st of March, 2019.

'Crossing the Threshold', poem for the celebration of the online graduation of DCU Nurses, Psychotherapists & Community Healthcare students, June 2020.

'Old Biddy Talk', poem film commissioned by the Department of Foreign Affairs to celebrate the first Brigid's Day, 2021.

'Sun Bath', *Local Wonders,* ed. Pat Boran, Dedalus Press, Dublin, 2021.

'The Key', 'Runes', 'The Unbecoming', *The Stinging Fly,* ed. Cal Doyle, Issue 46, Summer 2022.

'The Lionhearted', *Reading Gender and Space,* eds. Anne Fogarty and Tina O'Toole, Cork University Press, 2023.

'The Poet's Funeral Mass', *Poetry Ireland Review,* Issue 138, ed. Nessa O'Mahony, 2022.

Milton Keynes UK
Ingram Content Group UK Ltd.
UKHW011006050424
440583UK00004B/45